Rear View Mirror

Stories from the streets and the night.

Tony Schumacher

Foreword.

It felt like the clock was having a long conversation with ten to eleven the night I picked up a firebomb of a pixie outside the Empire Theatre on Liverpool's Lime Street. I seem to remember it had been raining both on the streets and in my heart and I was starting to wonder if I was wasting my life, and my fuel, driving around with a succession of £2 fares that were barely managing to cover my coffee intake let alone my diesel.

The firebomb gave me the right name through the window and Angie got into my car and into my life.

"Where are we going?"

"Crosby." Came the reply, and I gave a silent cry of thanks to the gods of taxi driving for at last giving me a fare that would result in paper money.

Had Angie been going somewhere nearer you wouldn't be sitting there reading this, although chances are I'd be sitting here writing it.

The difference being, Angie gave me an audience. But that's not all she gave me, she gave me confidence, guidance, a kick up the arse and a column in the best magazine in the North West of England, Liverpool Confidential.

"Where've you been?" I asked to mask my excitement at finally getting into decent fare into double figures.

"Manchester, for an awards ceremony."

"Did you win?"

"Nah... We never bribed the judges like everyone else."

"What do you do for a living?"

"I edit a magazine."

"Oooh I write a blog, do you want to read it?" I could almost hear her eyes rolling in their sockets behind me but she took the blog name and paid the fare and went on her way.

Over the next few weeks I read the magazine, drove my cab and ignored my blog (I'd only written three pieces and it was slipping into the morass of half hearted blogs that litter the internet like leaves in the autumn).

Then one day I got an email that changed my life:

"Subject: Your blog.
Tony,
It's very very good. I really "enjoyed" your domestic violence tale.

How would you fancy doing the occasional column for us? I'm sure it would be well   read/commented on.

Angie
Angie Sammons,

Editor,
Liverpool Confidential"

I still drive a cab for a living, but now I'm a writer, and I hope you enjoy what I've written.

Oh and by the way... Thanks Angie.

Tony Schumacher

April 2013.

About six years ago my life was going swimmingly. I had the lot. I had the wife, the son, the house, the career, the car and even the trendy dog.

Today? Well I haven't got the house, the car, the job, the son, or the career.

Even my dogs died.

I'm a living walking country and western song.

Let me explain; I was a Policeman. I wasn't an ordinary policeman; I was the type who did a bit of stand up comedy on the side. My life was filled basically with moments of fear, fighting, arguing and adrenaline, and that was just the comedy.

In the police I was a response officer, I basically used to drive around Liverpool with blue lights flashing answering 999 calls. I've kicked in more doors than Jack Regan and turned over more bodies than Quincy. It was messy, bloody, dangerous and at times, desperate. And I loved it.

I loved my colleagues, I loved the charging around shouting, I loved the challenge and I loved the thrills. I loved my life.

I honestly used to pull up at my house of a night, in my quiet cul-de-sac, and sit for moment and think about how lucky I was. I know that sounds crazy when you say it out loud, but I did. I was that happy.

Or at least I thought I was.

Six years later, sitting here writing this, it seems like someone else's life I'm writing about, I'm not sure of I'd recognise the bloke who used sit smugly in his car looking at his house with his gorgeous wife waving through the window. To be honest, if I met him, I'd probably think he was a bit of a kn*b.

That bloke's life finally fell apart when he found out his son wasn't his. In fairness, although he'd not noticed it, his life had been in trouble for a while but, like a carrier bag that splits at the bottom and drops your spuds on the floor all at once, I/he just hadn't noticed it going.

I'll not bore you with the details, that's another story for another day but, six months after my carrier bag split, I found myself without a job (never write a resignation letter when you are crying) and sitting in a rented house I couldn't afford with a designer dog that was, quite frankly, disappointed in me.

I had to do something, so when a mate suggested getting a cab drivers licence to "tide you over till you get your head straight" I decided to do that, if only to get out of the house that had become a prison, and to start talking to people again.

It was the best thing I've ever done. Because amongst the drunks, the drug addicts, the lager, the lovers, the lost and the lonely... I found myself.

It happened at about four am, sitting in a park, eating a lonely service station sandwich and staring at a cat getting beat up by a bird, that I decided to write.

And that cat, and that bird, led to my book *Rear View Mirror* being released about two weeks ago for the Amazon Kindle and if I ever meet them again I'll shake them by the paw/claw.

I'd never written anything before, so I was surprised at how good I felt when I wrote that first story. I didn't just feel happy, I felt different, like something had happened in my head and my heart, like a place had been found and that I'd come home. I remember reading it a few times and smiling to myself. I even printed it off and stuck it by my bed to read when I woke up, just in case in the morning, after the shine had worn off, I found it was rubbish. I've still got that original story upstairs, and I still don't think it's rubbish. I created a blog, and posted the story up there, and told what remained of my friends on facebook. Some of them read it, a few of them commented, and I felt good for the first time in years, so I wrote another one, and another one, and another one.

And I felt better; little by little, I felt better.

A few months later a lady got in the cab and we chatted and she told me she edited a local magazine. I told her I wrote a blog about the cab and she promised to read it. I didn't believe her. A few weeks later I got an email, and she said some nice things and offered me a column in the magazine and said she would pay me for the stories.

I still didn't believe her, but it turned out she was telling the truth. I'd become a writer, and I was happier than I'd been in years, and it wasn't money, it wasn't a house and it wasn't a car that was making me happy... it was my heart.

Which was finally fixed.

1. The Day After Father's Day

My Father died not wanting to make a fuss. At about three am on the 2nd march 1987 he woke up, got out of bed, put on a pair of trousers and a shirt and then crept downstairs so as not to wake my Mother.

He must have sat there for a while wondering what was going on, in his "Dad's Chair" by the fire. Looking around the living room for which he'd worked so hard, at the pictures on the sideboard of the family he cared so much for and maybe the air bubbles in the wall paper he'd spent so long trying to smooth away.

Eventually the pain must have become too much and he swallowed his pride and woke my Mum.

They went downstairs and he returned to his chair, his condition worsened as my sister joined them.

By the time I was awoken ("Leave him, he's got work in the morning") I'd say he was half dead. When he finally agreed to an ambulance he was three quarters gone, and by the time they arrived... well I suppose you've got the picture.

I can remember sitting in the ambulance staring at my Mother as she clutched a lonely slipper she had picked up on the drive, and she, in turn, stared at his bare foot sticking out from under the blanket.

The ambulance crew worked like the heroes they were, shouting at him, pounding on him and listening for sound. But in truth they were like bailiffs banging on the door of an empty house, it doesn't matter how loud you knock. If there is nobody home... nobody will answer.

Later, as we sat in a curtained cubicle, silent, like mice cowering under a bed, listening to footsteps and watching shadows pass by. I wondered who would be the hand on the family tiller? Who would be the rock, the oracle, the joker, the handyman, the provider, and the person who was always behind you, no matter what?

Last night, over twenty three years later I was thinking about him again, not because it was Fathers day, he hated that ("Wasting money on cards! You shouldn't have bothered.") but because of a chat I had with a guy while I was working in the cab.

On Sundays, the car normally ends up smelling of one of two things. Roast Dinner or clean washing. Visits to Mum's by errant sons who have fended questions along the lines of,

"Are you losing weight? Is that girl not feeding you?"

Or

"Will you bring your washing? I'm doing mine and I need it to fill the drum."

Balanced plates covered in foil and bin bags of "Summer Fresh Lenor" socks and shirts normally fill the back seat as the passenger faces a gentle ribbing from his jealous cab driver (me).

Father's day normally adds sheen to this; glasses of scotch shared with the "old fella" work to soften the edges more than lenor. And nostalgic chats of football in the garden and learning to ride bikes can usually be coached with ease and filed in my notebook.

But the roast dinner balancing bloke who got in last night had a different tale to tell me..

"Been to the folks for Father's day?"

"No mate, just been to me Ma's for me dinner"

"Smells lovely"

"She does a boss roast; she always made sure we had a boss roast, no matter what"

"My mum always burnt the beef!"

"Beef? We couldn't afford beef! Me ma was on 'er own, we mostly just had spuds and cabbage swimming in 'gipo!"

We laughed and chatted about whose Mum did the best roast, and agreed to disagree. Then he told me that he wasn't seeing his kids that day due to them being with their Mum and "her fella",

"He's a sound lad, taking them to Southport for the day; he's got a car... I wouldn't have minded seeing them, but they put a card through last week."

We sat in silence as he fingered the foil and looked out of the window. After a while he returned and said,

"You got kids?"

"No mate, it's a long story and we're only going to Bootle."

"I love me kids me, but I do a bit of drinking like."

Now in my experience a "bit" normally means a "lot" and a "lot" normally means a melancholy meander through memories of being hard done too with injustice and loss.

But not this time, this time it meant a long hard stare out of the window and then more silence, until finally, he turned and said,

"Me dad was an alkey, he got off when we were kids, I think me Ma chased him, but she tells us he did one."

"Is he local? Do you see him?"

"I think he's dead."

The sadness of not even knowing if your Dad was alive or dead struck me; I wondered what it would be like to not know if there was full stop at the end of your relationship. Never knowing if one day a reformed soul would tap you on the shoulder and give you a hug and tell you he was sorry.

Would that be worse than the certainty of knowing that the man you knew and loved, the man who let go of the saddle as you rode your bike for the first time, wouldn't be there when you glanced back proudly?

I think it would.

Fathers day is good for business, not just for me, but for the pubs, restaurants, sweet shops and liquorish manufacturers the length and breadth of this country and beyond.

A day of hugs, back slaps, aftershave and ale. TV's topped with cards with footballers, speed boats and vintage cars racing down country lanes.

A chance to show him you care, without awkwardness and mumbles.

I'm glad my roast dinner nursing passenger got in the car late on Father's day and not the day before. Had he got in the day before we might not have chatted like we did, football would have held centre stage and manly banter about "Those useless overpaid lazy..." would have took up our time.

But the main reason I am also glad is because it meant I didn't have time to sit here and write this until the day after, because I think it's the days after Fathers day, the ones that take up the rest of the year, that are the really important ones.

The ones where maybe you should take the time to give him a hug or shout,

"Hang on" when he says,

"I'll get your mother" on the phone.

Those are the days that you should treasure, because you love him, not because you've bought him a card.

361 days a year (allowing for birthdays, Christmas day and cup finals) when your dad deserves a hug.

So give him one today, before it's too late.

I should maybe stop there, but in honour of my dad (who had a mischievous and eccentric sense of humour) I'd like to leave you with a smile.

I'd like to take you back to that curtained cubicle twenty three years ago. My older brother had arrived and us four sat shell shocked, cold tea was all we had to deaden the pain until a young, nervous looking Doctor entered the cubicle after fumbling with the curtains like Eric Morecambe on a Christmas special. He shook my mother's hand and using a clipboard as a shield took a seat,

"This is always very difficult, especially when your loss has come so suddenly."

My mother nodded and sniffed respectfully in the way that her generation did when confronted by a man in a white coat,

"But in this situation time is of the essence Mrs Schumacher, I'm sorry but I have a difficult question for you."

"Of course Doctor, please, just ask."

"Is there anything your husband would have wished to donate?"

My Mum stared at us for a moment then bit her lip and pondered this greatest of requests,

"He had those slippers Doctor, they were hardly worn"

My Dad would have laughed like a drain.

2. It's Only A Hug.

George Formby (one for the kids this) once sang a song called "Leaning on a Lamppost" (I'm guessing he sang it more than once but you get the point).

The song goes,

"I'm leaning on a lamp-post at the corner of the street,
In case a certain little lady comes by.
Oh me, oh my, I hope the little lady comes by.
I don't know if she'll get away, She doesn't always get away,
But anyhow I know that she'll try.
Oh me, oh my, I hope the little lady comes by,
There's no other girl I would wait for, But this one I'd break any date"

Now, looking at this today, 70 odd years in retrospect, I think it would be fair to say that this would now be considered as tantamount to harassment. At the very least it would be sufficient evidence to present to a court as grounds for an injunction.

Poor old George would be signing the register for the next eighteen months under the firm instruction that if found loitering near any street furniture in the future, he, and his little stick of Blackpool rock, would be slammed into goal pending psychiatric reports.

That is of course, if he hadn't already been questioned by the Police at the scene after they had him open his ukulele case and empty his pockets on the bonnet of the Police car.

"We need your name for the stop and search form."

"Oooh mother! Turned out nice again!"

"Just your name sir."

"Hey hey! Never touched me!"

"Are you alleging we have assaulted you sir?"

Etc etc.

Why the hell am I writing about George Formby?

Good question.

It's just that the other night I saw someone leaning on a lamppost (it was halfway down a street), it wasn't George, although it was a little lady.

She and a male friend had walked past the cab while I was doing the crossword in the paper. It was a warm night and I had the windows open and the radio off.

Sitting in town inside a darkened cab is a unique experience, the world passes you by and plays out a million scenes and it's difficult not to feel a bit like a bird watcher in his hide sometimes. This was one of those occasions.

The young couple, who sounded like they were from out of town, maybe students, were having a domestic. They were both drunk, and I mean *drunk,* and it sounded like one of those pointless arguments drunken people have,

"Leave me alone!"

"I haven't done anything."

"Leave me alone, just go away!"

"Okay, suit yourself!"

"Where are you going?"

"You told me too..."

"I don't want to talk about it! Why did you do it?"

"I thought..."

"Leave me alone."

The young lad, was truly exasperated, his flopping hands and confused sighs made him sound like an Ivor The Engine tribute act ("Tonight Mathew I am going to pull Jones the steam out of a hole!") and the poor girl truly did not know which way to turn. She spun and pirouetted torn between walking away and carrying on the fight.

Now I don't know what had taken place, for all I knew the young lad had been playing trouser trumpet with her best mate, or maybe it was just a case of the vodka shots doing the adding up for her,

Vodka shot "So two and two makes eight."

Girl "Are you sure?"

Vodka shot "Yep."

Girl "It's just that I seem to recall..."

Vodka shot "Look, do you want me to do your adding up for you or not?"

Girl "It's just that I thought..."

Vodka shot "Look love, I don't have to do this you know? I could be just getting on with making you sick."

Girl "I'm sorry, so it's eight then?"

Vodka shot "Eight it is, you don't want to let him get away with it, I'd have a fight if I was you. Would you like me to look after your emotions and tear ducts?"

Girl "Do you mind?"

Vodka shot "It's all part of the service! That's what you are paying £1.50 for!"

Eventually our young lad had enough, he flapped his hands one last time and let out an almighty sigh and said those words we have all said at some point in a relationship

"I give up!"

He turned and wobbled off back to whence he had came.

Poor drunken girl let out a little whine (not Lambrini, hers was the plaintive kind that comes from confusion and desperation, normally as a result of actual wine (in my limited experience)).

She did that Hollywood thing of putting the back of her hand against her forehead and looked up and down the road for answers (or maybe a hackney cab) and then flopped against a lamppost.

She hugged the lamppost for a moment and had a little cry, the lamppost did that British thing of pretending not to notice (had it had hands I'm guessing it would of almost patted her back and then thought better of it and just stood there staring into the distance whilst it's shoulder got wet (assuming of course lampposts have shoulders)).

The girl realised how daft she looked and pushed herself away from the lamppost and gave it a little slap. She took a few paces and then turned to look down the road in the direction that her friend had gone (the lad not the lamppost) and gave another little plaintive whine.

Young lad was nowhere to be seen. He'd headed off toward the bombed out church no doubt muttering to himself about how unfair life was and whether he should get a burger or a kebab.

Drunken girl stood forlornly, rested her hand on the lamppost again and then wobbled off in the opposite direction to her erstwhile boyfriend.

As she weaved her way she cast the odd glance over her shoulder and it struck me that she actually just wanted a hug. Not from the lamppost but from her drunken lad. She stopped a couple of times, just her and her reflection in empty shop windows, both watching to see if he would come.

He didn't.

She looked at herself in the window a couple of times, but a hug wasn't forthcoming from that direction either.

Eventually she turned a final time and off she went, homeward bound to a wet pillow and a hangover.

I shook my head (I do a lot of that) and returned to the crossword as peace returned, I'm a firm believer that "Quick Crossword" is actually short for "Quicksand Crossword" because I usually get stuck and end up needing help. So as I chewed my pen and settled into deep short sighted concentration I got quite a fright as young drunken lad jogged past my window.

Drunken girl was long gone, I'd managed two answers so at least ten minutes had passed but he jogged on in what appeared to be a lost cause of catching her.

He didn't have his burger, his arms were empty, I hope he caught her up and filled them.

3. The Cat The Tree And The Bird.

I watched a cat get beaten up by a bird one morning; well I say it was beaten up. It was more sort of knocked around and chased a bit. But if I started with "I saw a cat get knocked around a bit by a bird the other morning" it would have lacked impact and you may not have read this far.

Assuming of course, that you have.

Maybe I'd be better off telling you what actually happened. I'd been working all night, ten hours with a little break in the middle to chill out. Well the night had been pretty busy and I'd pushed on through till about five thirty in the morning when hunger and thirst forced me to "have a mo".

I popped into the garage on Smithdown Rd (which is staffed by the most cheerful attendant you are ever likely to meet at five thirty in the morning. This guy asks how you are, talks about the weather and gives you that rarest of things... an early morning smile with your change).

I bought a dodgy sandwich and a bottle of water and drove around Sefton Park and pulled over by Greenbank Drive.

The park is always gorgeous, but especially so at that time of the morning, it tends to have a will 'o the wisp look to it, grey and green with a tiny gap in-between where occasionally, if you are lucky, you'll see a fleet fox splashing a dash of red.

I sat, door open, late night radio chatter extinguished and replaced with yawning birds and distant tyres. I sniffed my sandwich (I wasn't going to leap straight in) when out of the corner of my eye I saw a cat sitting under a tree watching me. It was about thirty foot away and seemed to be "having a mo" also.

Out of nowhere (well actually out of the tree above but seeing as the cat wasn't looking, and is unlikely to be reading this I think it's fair to say as far as he was concerned it came out of nowhere) a massive blackbird swooped down and quite literally knocked the cat over and then flew off.

Poor old puss jumped up and hopped around sideways a couple of times and then stopped and stared at me. Now I am no expert on cat body language but I know for a fact that cat was saying,

"What...the hell... was that?"

I smiled and shrugged and said out loud,

"You must be in his spec mate."

The cat didn't reply, he just glanced around and then regained some composure and sat back down. It was then, just as he nestled his bum back into its spot, when the bird came down and did it again, this time not just swooping, this time it did a bit of pecking and flapping its wings at poor old puss who was trying to get away and failing miserably.

Puss rolled and tumbled as the bird slapped and flapped a blur of yellow and black. The only sound I could hear was the rustle of the grass and beat of wings as the onslaught took place.

After a moment the bird flew back up into the tree and puss took a couple of steps away and sat back down, he was looking even more confused and maybe a tad embarrassed, I guessed if he'd been wearing glasses they would be twisted half around his head and that he would have scrambled to put them back on his nose to restore his dignity.

But cats don't wear glasses, so he didn't.

I broke off a piece of sandwich and held it out to him; I waggled the titbit and "puss pussed" a welcome and eventually he wandered over. Each step slow and nervous, until he sat about five feet away sniffing the air. I tossed him some tuna and he ate it and did that cat thing of not looking at you, in a kind of,

"Yeah, whatever." Feline sniff.

I tossed him some more tuna which he ate, and this bridged the gap between us enough for him to wander over and offer a faint nuzzle on the back of my hand. He stood and stared at what was left of my sandwich, pushing out his bony ribs to make a point, and I gave him some more, then he licked his lips, looked at the park and thought some cat thoughts, then wandered back to the tree.

I swear he almost sighed as he did so.

I felt sorry for him and said out loud as he went,

"She's not worth it mate."

But he didn't listen, cats never do, he just sat back down under the tree and watched me from there.

I drank my water and tossed what was left of the sandwich into a bin (best place for a Monday morning garage sandwich) and set back off for a couple more hours of work.

It was only when I was driving that I thought of the old lady and her husband who I met many years ago when I was a copper.

It was late night Newton Le Willows, probably about three am midweek. Now I think it would be fair to say that Newton Le Willows at three am isn't a hotbed of crime, it's more Dock Green than Hill Street, so any job that came out on the radio was seized as a means of staying awake.

A report came in from a neighbour reporting shouting from next door. I was the first car at the scene and after some concerted banging on the front door I was surprised to be met by an old bloke, about mid seventies wearing a pair of trousers, vest and braces. The trousers had once made up part of a brown suit, but now they bunched over his belly like a nylon Christmas cracker and his vest bore the grey of a thousand hot washes.

He ran his hand through his thinning grey hair that looked like it hadn't woke up yet, and told me everything was okay and the neighbour had been mistaken.

"It doesn't work like that I'm afraid," I said as I looked over his shoulder into the house, "I have to check everyone is okay mate, it'll only take a second."

His hand scrapped his hair again and it rose and fell like his chest when he sighed and stepped aside to let me pass. I smelt beer on his breath as I squeezed through the door but once inside the house smelt of polish, leather, gas fires and family.

I went into the living room; it was one of those that are full of brass, rugs and photos of grandkids in university gowns who never phone. Sat on a chair was a sparrow of an old lady. Pink flannel dressing gown clutched tight to her throat, furry slippers peeking out from its hem. The skin on her hands was wrinkled and brown and looked like half scraped wallpaper.

Those wallpaper hands were clutching a tissue to her nose and I could see it was red with blood.

I looked at the old guy, who had followed me in, his eyes flickered with sadness and shame and before he could speak I already had my hands on my handcuffs.

"You'd better put your coat on." Was all I said and he nodded sadly and did as he was told.

I drove him the three miles to the custody suite, he never spoke, and to be honest, neither did I.

The custody sergeant listened to my tale and politely asked the old guy for his details. The old guy stood still, did as he was told and called us both "Sir".

"Lodge him Shoey" The custody sergeant dismissed him with a wave of his hand and I led the old guy to his cell. At the cell door I waited for his shoes and the old man asked his first question of the night,

"What happens now sir?"

"I'll go get a statement off your wife, then I'll interview you, then the sergeant decides, do you understand?"

" I'm sorry son." He said, and for the first time his voice cracked,

"Don't be sorry, we'll sort it out."

"I just snapped."

"Don't tell me here, we'll talk about it on tape."

"There is only so much you can take."

"Don't say any more, I'll be back soon."

"Go easy on her."

I raised an eyebrow then shushed him again and closed the cell door; I made a quick notebook entry and then drove out to see his wife. When I arrived she had dressed and had fashioned her hair into one of those cotton candy ginger hair styles that only old ladies have. I followed her into the living room and she gestured for me to sit and offered me tea, I declined and pointed to the chair opposite for her to sit, in that way that coppers do in other people's homes.

Like we own it.

"So what happened?" I asked, pulling out a pen, all business with an eye on the clock,

"It's my entire fault."

"No, you mustn't blame yourself love, it's easy to blame yourself, you've been assaulted, nobody should have to put up with that."

"No, you don't understand, it is my fault, I started it, I always start it... he lets me hit him, I batter him... I've done it for years, I hate him for it, tonight he hit me back, he's never done it before."

To say that that wasn't what I was expecting would be an understatement. I was dumbfounded; I hadn't even clicked the end of my pen yet and the room had just tipped upside down.

She told me they had three kids and several grandkids, that they had been married for fifty odd years and that he had never raised a finger until that night. She told me that he had come home from the pub and fell asleep in the chair, that she had woke up and come down and that they had argued and that she had slapped him, then punched him then slapped him again, like so many times before.

And, this time, for the first time ever, he had slapped her back.

"I called him names, terrible names."

I looked at my pen for some help, but it just looked back at me.

"I deserved it, I wish he'd done it years ago, I'll not make a complaint, I'll tell them I walked into a door, you can't make me say anything."

There are times when you are a copper, and I am sure many police officers will have felt this way, when you just don't have a clue what to do next. And as I sat there that night on that couch looking at that little old lady who could have passed for tweety pies grandmother, and I didn't have a clue what to do next.

I can remember staring at my statement forms for a moment and then scribbling down some stuff about her not wishing to cooperate with the police. With hindsight, I maybe should have locked her up for assaulting him, she had just confessed to it.

But I knew that wasn't going to happen, I just didn't know why, was it too save my embarrassment or the old guys?

I told her I was going to go back to the station to speak to her husband and I left. She didn't see me to the front door, she stayed in the chair and I heard her sobbing as I stepped out into the street. Nobody else was out there to hear her, just me and the milk bottles.

At the time Merseyside Police had a zero tolerance policy when it came to domestic violence, an excellent tactic of everyone being arrested and interviewed which resulted in some good work being done. But as I sat opposite that gentleman, gentle man in the truest sense of the word, in the interview room that morning, just me, him, a duty solicitor and a tape recorder that picked up the solicitors every yawn in stereo. I felt like reaching across and giving the old guy a hug.

He was ashamed and tired and looked very very old.

I gave him a lift home so that he wouldn't have to wait for the buses to start and as we drove I told him what his wife had said, I told him he didn't have to put up with it. I told him about various charities that could support him and his wife to find different ways to communicate without violence, and, to be honest he didn't say that much back to me, he just stared out at the passing view thinking about the passing years.

As we pulled up outside the house he thanked me and said,

"I've put up with it for fifty years, there's not many left to go now, I'll be okay son, thanks."

He then got out and walked up the short path to the front door and disappeared inside.

The cat under the tree made me think of him, the cat could have just walked away and found another tree to sit under but it didn't. Something made it go back there and sit down and wait for the next onslaught from the angry bird.

It had the whole park to sit in, but that tree and that bird were where it had to sit.

Strange things cats.

4. My Favourite Trainers.

My mum bought my favourite trainers, which, in fairness, should deny them the right to be referred to as "cool" but it doesn't. They were the coolest trainers I had ever seen, electric blue nylon with three, yes three Velcro straps and a tan coloured rubber soul that didn't know when to stop. It rolled up over my toes like an Alladins shoe and back to the heel with a big flat flourish.

These were seriously cool trainers.

I remember opening the box and saying one word,

"Starsky!"

As I pulled them out and holding them up in the air, unbridled excitement before I'd even put them on.

When they went on things just got better,

"Look how high I can jump up in the air!" I shouted from the back garden, "They are so light I feel like they aren't there!"

When I discovered what they were like at stopping I had to run into the kitchen and skid to a halt on the lino,

"Look at how fast they stopped me! These are the best trainers ever!" I shouted before I ran off to do some more jumping.

When my mates saw them, Eddie shouted,

"They look like Starsky's!"

And I did a few skids/stops just to show how good they were at skid/stopping, and we all agreed they were the best trainers in the world.

"I don't even have to do up the laces! Look...velcro!" I shouted as I ripped and then smoothed the fastenings, "like astronauts have!"

"Wow!" someone shouted "You'll be able to take them off super fast! Just like Starsky!"

And I did a bit of jumping, really really high in the air, just to show how light they were.

I can remember not wanting to play football in them, I'm not sure, but I think I even considered taking them off so as not to get them dirty. Unaware of course, that nylon would have stood up to a hot wash in my mum's old twin tub no problem.

It was a long summer, I have a photo of myself wearing my trainers with a pair of flared jeans and an orange snake belt. My hair is long but shows the hallmarks of a mothers trim with its wonky fringe and sticky up back. My skinny bare chest can hardly be seen behind the swing ball bat I'm holding in front of me and the garden grass is worn down by the millions of skid stops and long jumps I must have done all through July.

I'm at the age when a skid stop is what I do on the stairs when I realise I've forgotten what I went up for (assuming of course I can manage to get up enough speed to force a skid) so I had to reach for my reading glasses when I took a look at that old photo this afternoon.

I smiled at myself and wished I'd known me back then, wish I'd known about some of the twists and turns that would lead me to be squinting at the past before they'd happened so that maybe I could have taken them differently.

But you can't skid and stop life.

I reckon it was only a few days until we met Paul on the back field, from a distance he looked like he was wearing pumps that looked a bit like the ones we had to wear in the gym in school. I couldn't wait to skid/stop in front of him to show him my new ones. I ran over and when I got close I saw his weren't pumps, they looked a bit like shoes,

"What are they?" Said Eddie.

"Adidas Samba, I bought them yesterday." Paul said, languidly, well as languidly as a 12 year old boy can be.

"You bought them?"

"Yeah, out of my birthday money."

All the others gathered around and I'm not sure but I think I may have jumped up in the air a bit and mentioned something about Velcro, but they'd gone. Gone to the land of "buying your own clothes" and looking cool.

As the summer passed my trainers faded slightly, and blue never looked as electric again.

5. She

She darted out from the side of the house, a pyjama clad wisp flitting through the sodium lit night throwing furtive glances back at the darkened windows of the sleeping terrace she called home.

I watched as she reached the garden gate and carefully closed it behind her, careful not to make a sound.

She climbed into the backseat and whispered her destination, and as we pulled away she craned her neck to look out of the back window like an actor in a sixties spy B movie.

"Aren't you a bit old to be running away from home?" I asked when she finally let out a huge sigh and settled back into the seat.

"I need a bank on the way." Was all she said by way of reply, cutting me off before I'd even got going.

We drove to Old Swan and I sat and waited as she used the cash point. Mine was the only car to be seen, silent early morning streets are the luxury of the cab driver and the urban fox, both living off kebabs and fretful daytime snatched snoozes disturbed by the sounds of the city.

I rubbed my eyes and listened to the bleeps of the cash machine, like the fox my ears twitched waiting for the reassuring sound of the money slot coughing up. It paid out and I relaxed a bit, no awkward conversations about funds when she got back in.

The back door opened and closed and we set off again, no sigh this time, maybe she'd been worried about awkward conversations as well.

"Oh god, I can't believe I'm doing this." She said.

I glanced in the mirror and saw that distance from the house had relaxed her stretched nerves and now she was calmer, head rested back onto the seat she was slouched sideways on, making herself at home.

"What's going on? I felt like Michael Caine in the Ipcress file when I pulled up then!"

My mention of old films and older actors made little impact on her, she only looked about twenty five and she puzzled at my reflected eyes and tilted her head, confused.

I'm down with the kids me.

"I'm going me fellas, can I smoke in here?"

"No, smoking is both bad for you and bad for my bank account. How come you are going your fellas now? It's quarter to four in the morning."

"Me mum doesn't know I'm seeing him, I had to sneak out."

"Sneak out? You're a big girl; you shouldn't be sneaking at your age."

"I'm, only seventeen, she'd batter me if she knew."

It was my turn to look puzzled in the mirror, I studied her. Dyed blond hair held up tight by an elastic band stretching her face. She wore no makeup and the only colour on her papery skin was the two grey blotches under her eyes. She wasn't pretty, but she could have been, in another life.

"Can you turn up the heater, I'm freezing?"

I turned up the heater and she shivered theatrically and pulled her stick thin arms across herself to keep warm.

"So what makes him so bad your mum doesn't want you seeing him?"

"He's been in prison."

"Oh dear, a bad lad eh?"

"He's a very bad lad, me mum hates him, proper hates him."

"I know I am starting to sound like your old fella, but maybe your mum has a point?"

She wasn't cold anymore but she kept her arms pulled around her, I had a feeling it was the closest thing she had to a hug.

"I've been with him for four years, it's hard to just blow him out."

"How long was he down for?"

"He got two years, but he only did one."

"Do you mind me asking what he did?"

"He battered me dad, he ended up with metal plates in his face."

I looked at her long and hard in the mirror and she shrugged back defiantly, both of us knew what the other was thinking and neither of us liked it.

"A bad lad indeed." I said to no one in particular and no one in particular answered.

She looked away from the mirror and studied her phone screen and we drove on in silence for a while, I cast the odd glance at her handset lit face. She wasn't texting, just reading something on the screen. I wondered if it was a text declaring love from her angry young man. She glanced up at me,

"You must hear all sorts in this car, people must tell you everything."

"People find the back of my head very soothing, it's either that or the honesty scented magic tree hanging in the boot."

"What's the maddest thing you've heard?"

"I had some thick bird in who told me she was going out with some lad who had battered her dad, that was pretty mad."

"I'm not thick! You cheeky bastard!" She laughed, for the first time that night.

I pulled a "not quite sure I believe you" face and she suddenly leant forward in-between the front seats and nudged my shoulder,

"Ee are, look at that." She proffered her skinny arm and pulled up the sleeve of her pyjamas. I looked down at her wrist and at the tattoo that ran up her inner forearm. It looked fairly new, and was written in the kind of swirly hand writing a Victorian might anoint a watercolour picture in a botany book.

"Love and pain." she said as I read it.

"Love and pain." I said in return.

She sat back in the seat proudly, like a little girl who has just told you she is four and three quarters. Proud as punch.

"There's no love without pain." She said with a certainty that made me sad.

"There is love without pain," I said, in a not so confident voice, "isn't there?"

"People always let you down, or go away, tell a lie or fuck things up. Always, it's just what people do." She flopped back into her seat and returned to looking at her phone, conversation over.

I thought about arguing the point with her, but I found that certainty disconcerting; now it was my turn to not know what to say, a seventeen year old girl had just taught me a life lesson.

We pulled into her boyfriend's street. It was a cul de sac of terraced two up two downs, yellow bricked and steel shuttered, the majority stood empty. Waiting for a demolition firing squad to exact the planner's verdict, death on a winter's morn.

Her boyfriend sat on his front step smoking a joint, I could smell it even though my window was up, he scowled at me through the smoke as he took a drag,

"You didn't tell me you were going out with George Clooney" I said as I scowled back.

She laughed and paid me and got out without saying goodbye. I watched as she walked around the car to George, who didn't take his eyes off me, one of those tough guys again, except this one had some homemade tattoos and a prison record to back it up.

"Well I've got central locking mate, do your worst."

He didn't stand and give her that hug; he didn't kiss her or hold her hands and ask her how her day had been. He didn't even look at her. She sat down next to him while he stared at me some more and then spat on the floor next to his foot.

Love and pain... maybe she had a point?

6. Let's Quit This Joint.

When I was a kid, I'm guessing it was around about 1972 or so, I remember walking to school one day in a horrible smelly thick fog. I can remember waiting to cross the road holding my mum's hand watching the cars creep past, headlamps yellow and muted like ghost ships lanterns in a film. I remember it was cold, and I also remember I didn't want to go to school (I never wanted to go to school).

I remember all of these things, but the thing I remember the most was the horrible smell. It clogged my nose and made me feel sick, it was a terrible heavy smell that seemed to slide down your throat and settle in your stomach like mercury in a bulb. I've often wondered if it was the last of the smogs that blighted our cities in the days before unleaded petrol and smokeless coal made our pollution see through.

There were a lot of smells back in the seventies, chip pans full of fat in the kitchen, cars that belched oily smoke at traffic lights, men used to have BO and didn't care, maybe because one bath a week was all you wanted in a house that didn't have central heating. My Mum smelt of Yardly and Blue Grass perfume, except when she came home from work, and then she smelt of Lemon Puff biscuits, which was always a bonus to a six year old.

I don't recall fabric softener called "Golden Orchid", in fact I don't recall fabric softener. Our soap tended to be a large green lump of brick and it was used on everything from floors to faces and it had edges that could slice paper for a week after it came out of the packet.

Now before this turns into an episode of all our yesterdays, what I am trying to point out is that smells are powerful things. Whether we realize it or not we live our life with them flicking neurons as we wind our way down the street. On a recent stroll through Huyton "Village" I savoured Sayers, KFC, Waterfields, Greenhaighs Bakeries and a fruit and veg stall (doing decidedly less business then the other shops I've mentioned above).

Above all of these high street aromas, the one which stood out more than the others was the smell of skunk cannabis. I counted it from different people four times, and not just the usual track suited monkey clutching his nuts either. In the queue in the bank I narrowed it down to two young mothers one of whom was smartly dressed and who appeared to be on her lunch from the council offices nearby.

Now I'm not some sort of narcotic prude, I worked in the Caribbean and Miami for a while in the early nineties; it would have been difficult to be judgmental when you are living with a Costa Rican during the heady days of Miami Vice on TV and Bobby McFerrin in the charts. But drug use was still a taboo, enjoyed in small trusted groups behind closed doors, like witches huddled around a cauldron some would share a joint, or very occasionally a line, most of the enjoyment would be the thrill of the forbidden, the risk of discovery, which was a good job, as most of it was dried oregano and talc. But users didn't care; thinking they were Tony Montana and living the dream.

When I got home from abroad I found an old friend had gotten involved in the heroin plague that had hit Liverpool after the riots, it had snuck up on him and slowly swallowed his life like a Python would a rat, he still hasn't fully recovered, we spoke a few months ago and he told me how he feared for today's youth and the casualness of skunk use,

"It's used so openly, I used to hide my drugs, now it's like sharing a bag of crisps."

In the cab I'll smell skunk three or four times a night, if I chat to the holder they will happily talk about it without a hint of shame, many will offer some gratis, like my dad might have offered a Trebor mint. Some will tell you they are dealers,

"But only so I can sort myself out without having to pay."

A few will mention they would like to stop, but not many, it's their drug of choice, and who am I to complain? Tony Montana, remember?

One Friday I dropped a particularly pungent passenger off in the Kensington area of Liverpool. Now Kensington (Liverpool) is a lot different from Kensington (London). It's a decaying Victorian area that was built to house the white working class who fueled the many factories that once surrounded it. Now the factories are gone, and, aside from a few stalwarts, so has the community.

Poor planning, poor housing and even poorer policing has left the streets of "Kenny" looking worse for wear, and the housing clearances that were both half hearted and half finished haven't helped matters much either. But my smelly customer didn't seem to mind this urban blight, he was too stoned to care. Both slow of speech and movement he lolled on the back seat oblivious to the decay, and the smell from his pockets which was so overpowering I had to ask him to open his window before my magic tree jumped out the car at the next set of lights.

After he left I opened the windows to air the car, mindful my next passenger didn't want to be stoned on arrival. I couldn't understand why the smell wouldn't clear until I realized I was parked near a pub where five people were smoking skunk whilst standing outside.

Two things struck me, the first was that they were prepared to observe the smoking ban, which carries an eighty pound fine, but not bothered by smoking a class B drug that could potentially result in five years jail time. Secondly it was only quarter to one in the afternoon on a weekday and they were in the pub and stoned, while I sat in a smelly car driving their dealers around.

I felt a bit of a mug for working to be honest.

All of this brings me, to a few months ago. I pulled up at a social club in Norris Green, it was late on a summer Sunday afternoon. A couple approached and gave the right name, and jumped in the back. They were slightly merry, and told me they'd been to a christening and had decided the night was young. It was one of those christenings that seem to happen now where everyone dresses like they are going to the Ascot races, posh frocks and suits from George at Asda.

Off we set and they chatted amongst themselves and I let them get on with it until I heard an almighty snort followed by a sniff from the lady, and then again, this time from the male, I turned my head to see what was going on,

"You okay back there?"

"Just snorted some beak lad , do you want a line?"

I told them I didn't and warned them they were getting kicked out if they did it again, they both gave genuine apologies, with the male saying,

"It was disrespectful of us, really out of order, I'm sorry, we've already had a few lines, it keeps us going when we are out you see?"

Not the most interesting of stories, it's probably played out in a million cabs every night around the world. But if I tell you they were both pensioners, at least late sixties in age. It was like catching Grandpa and Grandma Walton sitting on the porch in their rocking chairs sucking on their pipes, their crack pipes.

One wonders when it will be, or if it's already happened, that cocaine will replace skunk as a socially acceptable pastime to have on show to all?

Casual afternoon usage replacing a vending machine KitKat with your three o'clock cup of tea.

At least it doesn't smell.

7. Mind The Gap.

"Be careful it's easy to fall through the gaps." Was what a guy whom I used to work with once said to me.

We were replacing a ceiling and I was pushing it through into an empty room below, it was a dirty, dusty and tiring job in the days when bottled water came in old R.Whites lemonade bottles and health and safety meant a hankie over your mouth and everyone laughing when you fell off the roof.

Labouring was the first thing I fell into when I left school with two O'levels and a degree in indifference. It was 1983, Thatch was in Downing Street and wages, if they came at all, came in cash. It didn't take me long to realise I wasn't cut out for a life shovelling s**t. I spent longer telling jokes and stories than I did actually working; I was like some sort of camp entertainments officer, I think they only kept me around to maintain morale when we were all sitting in the back of the wagon driving to a job in the rain.

I've lost count of the number of places I've worked in since then, its well over thirty, I've driven forklifts, sold jewellery, been a barman, sailed the seas and even shovelled pigeon poo 125 feet up in the air (the pigeon had left by the time we got there).

The longest job I've done was also the toughest, the most rewarding, the most frustrating and the most depressing (even more so then shovelling bird s**t). I was a Policeman in Merseyside for eleven years.

I should explain that I'm no longer a copper, I loved the job but it took its toll and I sit here today as a writer and cab driver, there were many experiences and lessons learned in those eleven years, and I'd like to share one of them with you today.

I was working in the town of St Helens, specifically a place called Parr. A tough, deprived working class area that had been hit hard by the decline in the traditional industries of mining and glass making. The vast majority of people there were of good stock. Genuine and honest, they'd had it hard but bore their burdens with a good humour and a fortitude you could only admire. They tolerated a scouse copper in their midst as a necessary evil, and in return, I tried not to take the piss out of their accents too much.

Most of Parr was made up of small Victorian two up two down terraced houses, thrown up to shelter the masses that had arrived to serve the industrial revolution. Inside they were cosy and warm, many still had coal fires, and winter night statements would often be written against a background of popping crackling coal and ticking clocks.

Jack Russell's would eye me suspiciously as I took their place on the couch with china cups of tea balanced on chair arms with best biscuits on parade.

But it wasn't all "Lowry land", St Helens had once been home to Rainhill Hospital, in its day the largest "Mental Hospital" in Europe. Its many patients had long since been discharged to be "cared" for in the community, taking Tebbit's advice they had got on their bikes and instead of looking for work, they'd gone looking for help.

Some of them hadn't made it very far.

In one of those terraced streets stood a boarded up house, like a bad tooth it sat amongst its neighbours rotten and decaying. When I first started working in the area I'd assumed it was empty and waiting for redevelopment. But then one evening I was called to attend a report of "Youths causing annoyance" in the street where it was situated.

On arrival at the scene all was quiet, as was often the way when the job was over an hour old before I'd been dispatched. As a courtesy I knocked at the informant's door, an old lady answered and invited me into to a spick and span house. Pots simmering and washing drying the lady told me that she had rung because,

"The local kids are terrorizing Tommy."

"Who's Tommy?" I asked, as I dunked another bourbon and passed some to the jack Russell while the lady looked out of the window.

She pointed to the boarded up house opposite, I was amazed, it was the one I'd thought was empty for all those years.

She explained that Tommy had lived there with his mother and father all of his life until,

"He went t'upt Rainhill as a young lad" as she said this she tapped her head and looked up and left in that old fashioned way of not mentioning mental illness. She told me that Tommy had never worked, and that since his mother had died years before the house had gradually slipped further into disrepair.

"He comes and goes out back down t'entry for his bits o shoppin, poor beggar has kids kickin football gainst boards all times, day and night, tis a bloody shame".

I stood up and joined her at the window and stared at the old house opposite and promised to speak to him and to try to help him.

I then finished my tea, thanked her and stepped out the front door and walked across the road and knocked on what passed for a front door.

"Who is it?" eventually came from within.

"Police mate, can I have a quick word?"

"No... go away."

"Please sir, just a quick word, it'll only take a minute?

No reply.

"Sir?" Another knock.

No reply.

That was as far as the conversation went. My notebook lies open before me now, the words written down moments later, all those years ago. I see now that I posted my card through with a note asking him to ring me.

He never did.

About a year later, myself and a colleague where working night shift. It was cold, wet and as windy as hell. A quiet night and we'd mostly spent it splashing round silent streets watching the trees sway in front of street lamps as waves of cold grey rain had blown down even greyer streets pushed by the gales of wind.

We had been almost relieved to eventually get a job reporting "Suspicious Circumstances" and attended at the address within minutes. It was only on arrival I realised we were back at Tommy's.

An early morning passing motorist on his way to work had noticed that the front door of the house was hanging off and had phoned it in.

We got out of the car and true enough we found the door had fallen backwards into the hallway, it was difficult to tell whether it had just given up its draft excluding duties or if it had been forced. The wood was rotten and the hinges had given way and I guessed it was more the efforts of the wind than a burglar. I reached into the hall way and tried the light switch, it didn't respond. No electricity.

My colleague Steve fetched a powerful lamp from the car and I drew my torch and in we went. The short hallway was a mess, newspapers and bin bags were piled on the floor, once white paint work was thick with years of dirt and dust laden cobwebs hung from the ceiling like Tim Burtons Christmas decorations.

We shone out torches around the small space with disbelief, this place looked like a film set.

I had to push the living room door open such was the weight of detritus behind it. A narrow path led through piles of waste some of which was stacked head height. A solitary chair stood surrounded by rubbish and before it a small portable tv sat on the floor. We called out Tommy's name but he never answered.

We moved through the kitchen, and along with the smell a sense of foreboding grew around us. The kitchen was, unsurprisingly, a tip. Rotten food lay about and empty tins littered the floor and worktop. I noted an old water boiler and cooker that George Stevenson would have recognised. No glass was in the kitchen window and the rain and wind blew in to shift the chip shop papers that littered the floor.

I shone my torch through the window out into the yard, it too resembled a tip. Piles of bin bags several feet high lay all around; I guessed there were more rats out there than medieval London. I gulped and shone my torch around the kitchen floor and then shook my head at Steve who nodded a silent reply.

This wasn't looking good.

We called out again and set off upstairs. It's a horrible feeling climbing stairs in a house like that; you are praying you will hear a reply to your shouts as you tentatively sniff the air for a whiff of deaths aftershave.

Tommy didn't reply.

Two doors, two Bobbies. Russian roulette and you are praying you won't lose. I got the bog, except it wasn't a bog, it was a back bedroom that had assumed the duties. It was horrendous, I'll say no more.

Steve got the bedroom,

"Shoey! He's here." Came the shout.

I entered, Tommy lay in the bed, and all I could see was the top of his head. He was buried under coats and blankets and clothes. It looked like he had piled them on top of him as he had gone to bed. Rubbish was everywhere, the wind whistled around the room from both the ill fitted boards on the windows and the partially collapsed ceiling above.

It was as damp and as a depressing site as I had ever seen.

"I'll blow it in on the radio; we need to get the Sarge and the doctor out." Said Steve, the standard procedure for finding someone in this condition.

I reached down and as Steve held the lamp I gingerly pulled back the bed sheets to have a better look at the corpse, which turned, opened its eyes... and screamed.

He wasn't dead.

Although I nearly was; from shock.

"Who the f**king hell are you?" Tommy shouted as a powerful lamp shone into his eyes,

"We are the police!" I yelled back, more in shock than certainty.

"What? Let me put my hearing aid in."

Tommy scrambled about in some rubbish and pulled out an old fashioned hearing aid that whistled when he put it in,

"What are you doing in my house?"

"Your door was broken we were worried about you." I replied, gradually recovering from the shock of speaking to a dead man.

"Get out! Get out of my house now! I don't want your help! Leave me alone!"

He got up from the bed and angrily backed us down the stairs, I tried to explain that we were there to help him but he refused all excuses, he even wouldn't let us help place his broken front door back into its frame. As soon as we crossed the threshold he grappled with it and pushed it back baring any further conversation.

Me and Steve stood in the street dumbfounded. We eventually started to laugh, more in shock than anything else and we climbed into the car and left.

Later, after the laughter had subsided we realised what a sorry state poor Tommy existed in. In an effort to help we compiled a report for social services detailing our real concerns for Tommy, we told them what we had found in the house, and our belief that he wasn't in a suitable position to look after himself.

Weeks later I received a call from a nice lady who told me that Tommy had refused all offers of assistance, and that social services were powerless to help him if he wouldn't let them.

He'd fallen through a gap. It's easy to do.

8. Bin Bag Black.

There is black, and then there is really black.

There is the black that is like a school blazer in July, faded by twelve months of sunshine and rain, shiny in parts and slightly grey at the elbows. It's darkness worn away by a year of climbing trees, hanging on the back of chairs and pretending to be a goal post.

Other blacks are just purple on an off day, like those delicate "black" roses they try to pass you off with, the ones were you can see the colour just below the surface, cheating its way out.

But the best blacks are just black.

Black with no depth, black that is almost invisible, difficult to focus on and cold to the soul.

The sort of black that sucks the light out of the air and makes you shiver at the thought of touching it. The blackness of a horse pulling a hearse, the blackness of the sea to a sailor lost at night, the blackness of a bedroom to a child awake at two in the morning or the blackness of an inky Mersey millpond slapping the concrete shore.

Bin bag black.

I spotted the bin bags in the path as I pulled up; they were dotted down the drive like those papier-mâché boulders they used to have on Star Trek for the aliens to throw at Kirk. They looked half full and strewn in a way that suggested they been tossed in anger, for a moment I thought I may have stumbled into a domestic with an errant husband collecting his life as he fled from his wife. But no sooner had I pulled up when the front door opened and my fare waved and mouthed the dreaded words,

"Two minutes".

Not for the first time in this job, my head sank to my chest.

I've never understood folk who will try to move house in a cab, once, many years ago, a lady asked me could she fit a two seater couch in the back of my car, I told her to,

"Hire a van love."

To which she replied squinting over my shoulder,

"Maybe I can get it on the roof?"

"It's not the Beverley Hillbillys love!"

"It's twenty quid for a man with a van."

"So you rang me?"

"I'm only going round the corner."

"You are going round the bend love, next time buy a couch with bigger castors... and an engine." I said as I pulled away.

This time I gathered myself, got out and opened the boot,

"Are there many more bags mate?" My spirits going down faster than the boot went up,

"Just this lot and two boxes in the house mate, I'm sorry I know it's a pain in the arse." He replied, and he meant it, I could tell by his face, this was a guy who was enjoying his task less than me.

I walked up the path and grabbed two of the bin bags, and, in best buy bin bag fashion, the first one split and gave birth to assorted socks and undies all over the floor,

"Oh for fucks sake" we both said as he peeled off another bin bag and we picked up the clothes,

"I didn't think this day could get any worse," he said as we tried to manoeuvre the old bag in to the new like two clumsy surgeons, "my missus has took the kids to her mums and left me too it."

"Moving house is always a nightmare."

"This is more than a nightmare," he said without looking at me, "we're being kicked out."

"Oh no, dodgy landlord?"

"Repossessed." He replied without looking up. "I've not worked in a year."

I looked at the top of his head for a moment and then returned to stuffing duty, unsure of what to say other than,

"Shit, I'm sorry."

"It's okay, glad it's over, not worrying now that it's over." He said, unconvincingly.

When we'd loaded the rest of the bags I followed him into the house to get the last boxes, I was surprised to see a dining table and three piece suite in a lounge an estate agent would soon be calling "light and airy".

"I thought there were only boxes left?" I said, nodding to the couch,

"We've got to leave it, no space at her mums, unless you want it?"

I shook my head and he looked around the room, his eyes seeing the memories he was leaving with the couch. The cuddles in front of the telly, the kids bouncing on it full of vim and vigour, the drowsy Sunday afternoons on its makeshift bed.

Now it just looked like a leather coffin the night before a funeral left lying in state in an empty parlour.

There is something sad about a house with no photos; they are like the tiny bits of DNA that turn it into a home. I could see the outlines on the wall where they had been, all that was left was grey ghost frames on white wallpaper, the pictures were long gone, like the wife, kids and laughter they'd once caught.

We picked up the boxes and took them outside to the car, there were no neighbours to wave goodbye as he pulled the door closed behind him for the last time, I wondered if they were watching through curtains and blinds, like bad actors in a western, embarrassed to say goodbye, to further the shame and highlight the pain that was written on his face.

After he told me where we going we didn't speak again, the journey passed in silence and sighs, and when we arrived at his mother in laws he insisted I dump the bags on the kerb saying I'd done enough, I think he just wanted me to go.

And in fairness, so I did, with a twenty pence tip that embarrassed us both.

Later, at about two thirty in the morning, I leant on a railing by that mill pond Mersey river, with its lusty slaps, like a pretty girl patting the seat next to her, urging you to sit down so you could look closely into her inky black eyes.

I wondered how tempting it must be for someone under the pressure of no work, no money and an unsympathetic bank to take up the invite.

I sipped some cold coffee and shivered against the oncoming winter, it'll be a long one, especially if you haven't got a home to call your own.

9. Stop and Stare.

My best mate lives in central London, a huge cacophonous clanging bell of a place.

Our daily phone calls are punctuated with sirens in traffic, the ebb and flow of passing conversations in a hundred different tongues, bleepers on bus doors and the crashes of cups and plates in busy cafes. He sails through it with a Zen like calm, aloof from what goes on around him, only occasionally needled by shouting kids on the back seat of a bus.

I don't know how he does it, at the end of our calls I normally need a moment to collect myself like Tom after Jerry has slammed some cymbals either side of his head.

Where I live it is about five minutes walk for me and the big daft dog to an insanely busy motorway junction. Every day I run the gauntlet of impatient drivers and kerb hopping cyclists (oh for some cheese wire). I often have to step aside for joggers in trances wearing iPods that remind me of the electrodes on Frankenstein's monster. Trucks drag trailers, inches at a time, hissing and sighing at the change of a traffic light, like kids in a queue at a funfair.

At the weekend motorcyclists career around, forty something men frantically chasing the thrills they miss from their youth, I tend to doubt they'll catch them, no matter how fast they go. But it gets them out the house, away from teenagers and wives, who may be happy to hear them roar into the distance.

I battle through this war zone because on the other side is my secret garden. A hidden footpath leads the way down the side of the motorway and through some dense trees to a country lane that goes nowhere.

The lane was made redundant by the motorway many years ago, cats eyes run down its middle waiting for headlights that will never come, and a moss covered road sign warns of a bend that has long since heard a screech of tyre.

Me and the big daft dog normally stop and say hello to the two horses that stand in a field. Maurice and Barry (it's a teeth thing) wander over when they see us coming, they stick their heads over the stone wall and wait for a nose scratch from me and a sniff from big daft dog. The dappled Barry often has cause to do a hop jump run thing when he sees us, it always makes me smile, it's nice to be the highlight of someone's day, even if that someone is a horse.

If I walk on, and I always do, by the time I've reached the stream with its bridge the sound of the motorway is long behind us. I once saw a Kingfisher flit over the water, an artists' brush with an electric blue flourish that took my breath away. I've never seen it again;

I tried to take its picture with my phone but was too slow. Like a ghost hunter I lack the proof of my visions, but the moment will live with me forever.

"Did you see that?" I said to the big daft dog, but he didn't answer, he never does. He just stood on his hind legs looking over the bridge, like always, trying to catch a glimpse of a squirrel or maybe a water rat. If he sees one his tale will frantically shout,

"Did you see that?" And if I'm lucky, I did.

We carry on past a corn field and up past the stables with the old guy who never says "Hello".

He always looks across and just raises a hand, never a word just a hand. In his other hand he carries his bucket, always his bucket, maybe he was born with it, along with his blue bib and brace and his silence.

I once watched him looking out across a field of young green barley; he stood still, with his bucket, for what seemed like an age, the barley was being caressed by the wind and dipped and swayed as if invisible angels where flying low, playing chase on a spring morning off.

When he saw me he raised his hand and tilted his head to the field, and I knew what he meant and watched it with him for a while. Although we were sixty feet apart we were together for a moment and I briefly understood why he never spoke, he didn't want to disturb the angels.

The big daft dog and I will turn and walk along the lane, and then through an old farm yard. Rusting machinery lies around, an elephant's graveyard with a stone barn that pines for its long lost roof like a bald man might for a perm.

A sharp left and we are in the fields, off in the distance I can see the motorway but if I turn my head, and I always do, I see only gently rolling fields.

In summer, if the winds blow, the corn moves like silk on a starlet's thigh, holding my gaze and making me stop and stare. No playful angels this time, the corn is yellow and crackles in the wind. Its heavy headed ears are nearly ready for the reapers scythe, which, when it passes will leave the field awash with broken stalks of stubble, and mice blinking in the sunlight.

Onwards to another lane that leads to another bridge. This one is modern and from its crest you can see Wales on a good day and Runcorn on a bad one, well... you can't have everything can you?

Last Saturday, during a rare day of daylight work, I picked up a little old lady in the city centre. I sat, waiting for her, surrounded by buses and cars, when she finally opened the door fumes and noise punched my senses like a stun grenade and she quickly slammed it shut and grabbed her seat belt tightly across her chest, a stressful day coming to an end.

"Ooooh." she exhaled, the hustle and bustle of a Saturday shop detailed in a drawn out sigh.

"Where too love?"

"Somewhere quiet." She replied quick as a flash.

Fifteen minutes later I dropped her at her house on Edge Lane. Now it's a long time since Edge Lane resembled anything like the Lane I detailed above, it thunders with traffic most hours, of a night its speed cameras flash more often than Paris Hiltons draws, but stand redundant in daylight as traffic inches past, a giant mechanical glacier.

"I don't know how you live here, what with all this traffic" I said as she collected her bags.

Someone gave me the finger for holding him up from pulling forward thirty feet. He "squeezed" past with three feet to spare and shouted something I couldn't hear, his mouth moving like a goldfish in a plastic bag.

Good job I don't do road rage.

"You get used to it," she said, but then paused, suddenly wistful, "I have to say though, it would be nice to go somewhere with peace and quiet every now and then, mind you, it's difficult to find anywhere like that nowadays isn't it?"

"Yes" I thought, "because I'm not telling you where it is."

10. A Friend in Need.

A friend asked me this week "How many friends do you have?", well, I say a friend asked me, I've never met her or heard her voice, for that matter I don't even know what she looks like. And when I say she asked me, what I actually mean is she tweeted me and the three hundred other people she "knows" on twitter.

We've had a few decent conversations in the past; obviously they have been limited to 140 characters or less, that and whether or not T-Mobile have turned the coat hanger they have for a mast near to where I live around to face my house, but other than that I think it's fair to say she is a friend, even though we'll never meet or actually converse face to face.

Thinking about it... for all I know she is a fat bloke in Wigan.

The whole friendship thing popped into my head again today when I was walking the dog, coming towards us was a lady I say hello to pretty much every day of the week. She takes her Jack Russell out at about the same time as I take the flea bag I live with, and our paths (and leads) cross on the main road close to where I live.

We normally stop for a moment, to allow for the sniffing of bums (the dogs that is) and to discuss the weather whilst ignoring the canine snorting ceremony in a terribly English way, fifteen seconds later we move on with a "Cheerio!" and a "ta ra!" (She's posher than me).

Today as we chatted about drizzle, her mobile rung and she answered with,

"I'm just chatting to a friend, I'll call you back."

I almost looked over my shoulder for her friend, then I realised she was talking about me. I don't even know her name and she called me her friend; think about that... how many friend do you have whose name you don't know?

We concluded our chat when she said,

"Better get on, I've got dancing tonight." She said, waltzing off.

I carried on walking pondering my new found "friendship" and the value of what we call a "friend". I thought about my best friend, he lives in London; we met on the first day of infant school in 1972 and we pretty much sat next each other in school right up to leaving in 1983 (except for one year that he won't let me forget, when I was stuck in the thick class because the teachers couldn't read my handwriting (not because I was thick, honest)). We travelled the world together working on cruise ships; Greyhound bused around the USA twice and once lived on a hotel roof at Miami airport for six days because we had no money. We normally chat a couple of times a day about nothing, he winds me up and I wind him up, when we meet we've been compared to a pair of old ladies bickering.

I love him, although I'd never tell him, because he is a fat idiot who gets on my nerves, and besides, just to confuse matters further, he isn't a friend he's a mate.

Now a mate is a sub division of friend, in many parts of the UK it would be considered to be lower down the pecking order than friend. But in Liverpool a "mate" is better than a "friend"; you would never hear a drunk with his arm around another bloke's neck saying,

"You're my best friend you are, I love you I do."

For that sort of drunken sentimentality only "mate" will suffice.

A mate will tell you things a friend will never do,

"He/she was never good enough for you."

"You've got bog roll stuck to your foot."

"There is a lump of food on the edge of your mouth."

Think about it, if it wasn't for our mates we'd all be walking around with bits of cornflake on our chin whilst the rest of the world pretended it wasn't there.

A couple of months ago two young female friends got in the cab as my hectic Saturday night shift was coming to an end. My heart sank as the bleached blond beached on the back seat and started to sob in a way only a forlorn drunk can do.

"Waaaaa haaaa haaa ha! Waaaaaaaaa ha ha ha!" She replied when I asked where we were heading,

"Maghull please." Replied her mate as she smoothed her friend's fringe from her sodden face.

"Waaaaaa haaaa haa ha!" Added chuckles as I turned up the radio and twisted the steering wheel,

"Is she okay love?"

"She's just caught her dick head fella kissing the face off some girl."

"Waaaaaaaa haaaaaa haaaaaa." Said her mate in agreement, head bobbing like an Iron Maiden fan during an encore.

"He's not worth it love," I said over my shoulder, "there's plenty more fish in the sea." I was now aware that I was starting to sound like I was reading from a book of "Cabby's Consoling Clichés" so I decided to shut up and leave them to it.

"Come here." Said her mate and pulled Blondie close, putting her arm around her and wiping her cheeks with a tissue. The gut wrenching cries of anguish abated to softer intermittent sobs and she rested her head in her mates lap and I breathed a sigh of relief I wasn't going to have to listen to her all the way to Maghull.

I lost myself in late night radio and route planning as we ambled on our way; it was only after a few miles I realised I could hear the sound of chuckling coming from over my shoulder. I watched the mirror as Blondie's mate whispered in her ear and smiled as Blondie giggled through the tears and nodded her head.

After a moment Blondie turned and said,

"I love you, thank you for making me smile."

I smiled again as they hugged and then sat in silence, hands held, friends forever, there for each other, thick and thin.

I might phone that fat idiot in London in a minute, maybe you should phone yours too.

11. Dandelions.

I've often wondered, what makes a weed a weed, and a flower a flower (shows how weird I am) I'm sure there is some sort of botanical definition to sort the wheat from the chaff (cereals now!)

I remember, a long time ago in a past life, many years and many miles before I sat behind this wheel and drove you home. I sat behind a very different sort of wheel, and back then if you were in my backseat I wasn't taking you home, I was taking you somewhere you probably didn't want to go.

No... I didn't work for a bus company, I was Police Constable 1774 of Merseyside Police. Honestly, I don't know how it happened either, but bear with me, because this week, that life, and this one crossed, and I'd like to tell you how.

I'll start back then.

I was out on patrol, window down, elbow at rest I was cruising around looking for trouble when my radio interrupted and sent me to look for a little boy who had gone missing, it was going dark, in that late summer creeping up on you sort of going dark way, where the horizon is coming closer and the days detail is starting to fade.

His mum had phoned the control room franticly after shouting for him in the back yard and then finding the gate open when she had gone to look.

The sun had dipped and the sky was turning pinky blue when I spotted the little fella wandering in Sherdley Park. I shouted him and we walked towards each other, like mismatched gunfighters in a dodgy western, we met in the middle of an empty car park. Even his shadow was short and he toed the ground and didn't lift up his head, he smelt of cut grass and summertime as he told me his name nervously and wobbled his bottom lip as I gently admonished him for not telling his Mum where he was going. Sheriff Tony, the only law west of Rainhill.

He took my hand and we walked across to my car, I asked him where he had been. He reached into his pocket and pulled out a handful of dandelions, yellow and crumpled, looking like little sploshes of paint on a grubby palette.

The poor things looked like they also were missing their mother.

"I went to pick flowers for my Mam, cos she hasn't got any."

By this point it was my bottom lip that was starting to wobble

"Come on Sundance, get in the car."

"Can I play with the siren?"

"No."

"Why not?"

"Because you have to be very good to play with the siren."

"I'll be good."

"You have to be very very good for a long time to play with the siren."

"How long?"

"Well it took me twenty seven years before I could play with it."

"Twenty seven years? That's forever!"

"Trust me, it feels longer."

When we pulled up in his street, a small welcoming committee of anxious neighbours huddled around a tea cup clutching mum. They parted as I approached and for a moment I thought the whole street was going to burst into cheers and hoorahs (as a Policeman it's not very often people are glad to see you, so when you get the chance to smile on arrival you make the most of it).

I beamed.

"Where the f**k'ing hell have you been?" she screamed.

I stopped beaming and then realised she wasn't talking to me.

Me and Sundance glanced nervously at each other, I don't know who was holding whose hand tighter.

"What have I told you about going out of that yard without telling me?"

Silence.

"What have I told you?"

We all waited...

"Not to go out without telling you."

I breathed a sigh of relief; I was worried that if he couldn't remember we'd both end up having to write:

"I am not to go out of the yard without telling you"

One hundred times before she'd let me leave, and I was worried about the kebab in my hat on the back seat of the car, it was going cold. And trust me on this; there are few worse things than your hat smelling of kebab, especially when it starts to rain. Just trust me.

His mum held out her hand and I transferred ownership of Sundance to her, he knew what was coming as she pulled up on his arm and made ready to smack the back of his legs, he dangled like a conker going up against a cricket bat. Mum made ready and neighbours nodded like an angry posse looking for a lynching.

But little Sundance had a trick up his sleeve, or rather his tracksuit pocket, he deftly dug and like a slightly taller Paul Daniels he magically produced the dandelions and thrust them in his Mum's direction

"I was getting you some flowers!" he howled, waving his desperate pardon frantically above his head.

A massed chorus of "Aaah" went up and Mums hand hung in the air like an executioner's axe waiting for a priest to finish a prayer.

Little Sundance spun on tip toe in the wind. He waved the weeds in his outstretched hand pleadingly at his Mum, I willed a stay of execution, as did, I believe, the posse, almost as much as little Sundance did.

If there had been a church bell it would have sounded as Mum whacked a stinging slap onto the back of his legs

"Don't give me that "brought you some flowers" s**t you little bas**rd! I wasn't born yesterday!"

Slap.

"You told me that..."

Slap.

"Last..."

Slap.

"Time..."

Slap.

"You went missing you..."

Slap.

"Little sod!"

One final slap on the legs drove the point home.

Sundance wailed and the posse shook their heads, he'd been found out and the walk of shame up the short path was a painful one punctuated by yelps, skips and tears.

The door slammed and I stood in the street, like a bounty hunter who'd tracked down the guilty but felt a bit guilty himself.

I thought of little Sundance the other night, I had a slightly older Sundance in the car. Instead of dandelions he was clutching a carrier bag full of fish. Yes, fish. Judging by the hour, and the inebriation of the carrier of the carrier I'm guessing that the fish had been bag bound for a while...

"Jesus Christ mate! Open the window!"

"Yeah sorry lad, got some fish for me bird like."

"What is she? A penguin?"

"She'll be like Emu if you don't get me home soon."

He hung the bag out of the window as I drove, I kept glancing in my mirror expecting to see a stampede of cats setting off the speed camera on Scotty Rd.

"Have you been out all day?"

"Yeah... ow'd you know?" he slurred,

"Well judging by the smell of the fish, I'm guessing they aren't still wet from the sea"

"Deese? Deeses are a present for 'er like."

"Is it valentines already?"

"When you've bin married as long as I ave lad, you lern neva to go 'ome widout a prezzie, e'specially if you've bin on der lash... which I ave like."

He added, just in case I hadn't noticed.

I thought there was a twisted logic in what he was saying, just like the dandelions maybe the fish would soften the blow (definitely if placed down the back of your pants, but let's be honest, that would be worse than your hat smelling of kebab).

We pulled up at his house.

"I've gorra go get der money, do you want me to leeve deese fish ere?"

"Good god no!"

He got out and wobbled up the path, tucking his pungent parcel under his arm, I didn't know who I felt sorrier for, the fish or the arm pit, he wobbled and fumbled with his key and his pocket, but before he reached the door it opened and his wife greeted him lovingly,

"Where the f**king hell have you been?"

"Ah aye girl, I bought you some fish."

"Ger in gobshite while I pay the cab."

I was there all over again, the bounty hunter, waiting for his pieces of silver, palm outstretched, the killers collection plate.

"Jesus Christ lad, it stinks of fish in der." Was all she said as he thrust me my fiver,

"The hell it does." I replied.

12. Date night.

A Tuesday night is normally student night, noisy young things full of vodka and dreams singing along to the radio (which can be off putting when its Talk Sport) generally having a good time whilst reminding me I'm getting old.

Now please understand this won't be a usual cabbies moan about "bloody students". I like them, they are always handy for topping up your small change levels and so far, none of them have ever tried to rob me (so far).

I enjoy listening to them talk about what they will get up to that night, how so and so fancies so and so, so and so slept with so and so, and so and so has caught something off that dirty so and so who slept with so and so.

The majority are bright young things who have the whole world (and the odd clinic) to look forwards to and you can almost smell the optimism (with the chicken burgers and kebabs).

They drift through university chasing dreams and each other like rabbits in a carrot field with few concerns about what the future will bring, and I for one am jealous that I can't have my youth one more time so I could gloriously squander it all over again.

I pulled up at an ugly house, stared at an old front door, and willed it to open. The clock ticked and my fingers tapped until eventually a lovely young girl emerged like a colourful butterfly from a dirty grey cocoon.

She stopped on the step and fumbled with her bag, nervously waving for me to wait as she somehow dug deep in the tiny clutch looking for something, maybe my lost patience.

I sighed.

She finally found what she was searching for and clip clopped down the short path on heels like six inch nails. When she got in the car she flustered and flapped at the long dark hair that framed her face with her furrowed brow.

"I'm sorry, I just need to check..." her well spoken voice trailed off and I glanced at the clock for sympathy but didn't get any.

Time marched on and she gabbled away more to herself than me,

"Sorry, I'm not sure I've got everything."

I looked in the mirror as she rifled through the bag again,

"Just take a deep breath and relax love."

She glanced up and smiled, hands full of cash card and mobile phone,

"I'm a bag of nerves, sorry."

"Just relax and stop saying sorry."

She smiled a lovely smile, the sort that made me wish I was twenty one again, and put the bag on the seat.

"Just take me to town please."

"Good idea, whatever you've forgotten you won't need, unless it's the money for the taxi."

She laughed, apologised again, then went onto explain,

"I'm going on a first date."

Now I love it when someone tells me something like that, to me it's the gold standard of conversation material. As a cab driver I'm always desperate to grab onto a chat that pulls me away from the usual topics of the football or "Have you been busy?" variety.

So I dived right in,

"Wow! Where did you meet him?"

"Well I haven't yet."

"Really? A blind date!"

"Well not really... I'm a bit embarrassed to say, but I met him on a dating website."

I made all the usual noises about "oh don't be daft" etc. But I was actually quite shocked. A young pretty girl, at Uni, on a dating website? I thought dating websites were basically for losers like me, not for young people living their dreams. I asked why she was using a site to meet guys and she replied,

"I had the same boyfriend since I was thirteen, nearly seven years. We finished when I came here because he didn't like me going away to study. We lived in a small village and everybody just sort of hooked up when we were young. I don't like being on my own and I didn't know what else to do, I've never really been on a date or chatted to a guy in the pub. This is so new to me."

Now I knew why she was nervous! A first date at the age of twenty odd must have been a nightmare. The last time someone asked her out she was on her way home from buying "Bunty" after a hard days skipping. And here she was, in the age of Sex In The City and BBC Three nervously telling me that she had all the experience of a Jane Austin character in the ways of modern dating

"Are you married?" she asked,

"No, It's just me and the dog, and to be honest he's on the lookout for his own place." I replied,

"What do you talk about when you go on a date?"

And it suddenly struck me, there was I feeling sorry for her and the last topical conversation I had on a date was about the poll tax riots.

I smiled thinly in the mirror and tried to appear like I knew what I was talking about,

"Oh I gab about anything, just be yourself," (I'm all for honesty in the cab, but not from me), "he'll be just as nervous as you are."

She nodded grimly; unaware she had just taken dating advice from someone who eats cornflakes in his pants on the couch whilst listening to the Archers.

"I hope it goes well, I don't like being on my own." She said sadly to the window and my heart broke as my throat choked and I hoped it went well for her too.

We soon arrived at her destination and her nerves bubbled back to the surface as she flicked at her hair and clutched at my arm,

"That's him, what do you think?"

I looked across the street to the young lad who was pulling at his sleeve and looking up and down the road, he looked like he was about to faint.

"He looks a bit shifty to me, too young for you by far." I winked and she laughed and squeezed my arm again.

"Thank you." She smiled,

"No, thank you." I replied, realising that if I'd been twenty one she would have been out of my league anyway.

She opened the door and took a deep breath then was gone.

It was lovely watching her head toward him and to watch him smile in that way that blokes do when they can't help it, big and broad.

He held out his hand, awkward and unsure, and she took it and pecked at his cheek and I thought I saw him blush as they turned to go up the steps to the bar. Before she went in she glanced back to me and gave a little wave and like a dope I waved back and gave her a thumbs up as they disappeared.

I felt like a father must do when he sees his daughter walk down the path with a scruffy young oik for the first time, almost shouting,

"Make sure you have her home by half past ten!"

But she was gone and I'll never know how it turned out or what time she got in. I hope it went well; the world deserves a bit more love in it.

Now, what does "non smoker gsoh own car, must like dogs" sound like?

13. The Kiss.

"Are you alright mate?"

I said to the bedraggled moaning wreck in the mirror (it was my rear view mirror, not the face I see every morning when I crawl out of bed). The shadowy lad on the back seat took his head out of his hands, wiped his wet hair from his face and nodded,

"Sorry mate, yeah I'm fine."

"If you want me to stop just say."

"No, I'm okay; I've only had a couple of drinks."

I eyed him suspiciously as he rubbed his face again with both hands and let out another almighty sigh then leaned back in the rear seat and stared at the roof of the car.

"Are you sure you are okay? You're making me nervous here."

He looked at me and smiled thinly with a hint of apology,

"I'm really sorry mate, I've had a fantastic night and I've just gone and made a massive mistake and I can't believe I've been so stupid."

We stopped at some lights and I watched him as he silently shook his head to himself, his long, wet, curly hair framing his face like malfunctioning curtains at a rundown theatre. The rain hammered against the windscreen and made the outside world look like a Monet painting as my wipers, like my passenger, struggled to cope.

I wavered, my writer's curiosity urging me to jump into his emotions and dig at his story only tempered by my driver's experience of engaging with emotional wrecks at two thirty in the morning.

The writer won... again.

"What's happened?"

He smiled and shook his head sadly and flicked at his dripping fringe again, took a deep breath and said seven of the saddest words I have ever heard in my life:

"I can't believe I never kissed her."

The lights changed and as the car moved forward the story moved back.

"I've been on a works night out."

"The old office romance? Trust me, I've done it and it only ever leads to problems."

"We work in a shop."

"Same principle, it's great at the beginning, but if things go wrong, which they are wont to do, you will soon find yourself hiding in the bog so you don't pass on the corridor. Next thing you know you are both in front of your line manager as he or she does their best Jeremy Kyle impersonation, you should be glad things went the way they did."

He shook his head and stared out of the window, no doubt thinking about how stupid the git in the front was. After a moment he sighed and made eye contact again in the mirror,

"It was her leaving do, she's gone, left the company."

"Oh."

"We've worked together for two years, been really good mates, I mean like best mates, do you understand?"

"Yes."

"I've always liked her more than that though, and I think she has always liked me more than that, but she has a fella."

"Ah."

"He's a tit."

"They always are."

"No he is! She tells me about him, he is a lazy get, never works, smokes weed all day, treats her like she is dirt, they never go anywhere they just sit all night in his mums watching telly."

He looked back to the window and rested his chin in his hand and shook his head at the rain and the night,

"Can't believe I didn't kiss her."

I waited.

"We work together, but we are always with other people, it's a busy shop but we have loads of fun, she makes me laugh loads, I'm really going to miss her, tonight we all went out because she is leaving."

"Where is she going?"

"She's got a manager's job in another company, on the Wirral, closer to where she lives."

I realised that was why, when I had pulled up, he had jumped into my cab and left her standing in the rain, she would have been waiting for a Wirral cab to surface out of the Mersey.

"Well the Wirral isn't too far; can't you get a job with her new company?"

It's a women's clothes shop, there is no chance."

I nodded and drove on; we both sat silent listening to the tyres splash through the grooves in the road made by the many others that had passed that way.

I thought about how they had stood waiting for the respective rides, when I had seen them, sheltering under a shared umbrella, I had assumed they were boyfriend and girlfriend. They had the closeness and easy intimacy that only lovers have in a storm. Drawn together under a nylon maypole, arms linked and shoulders touching, faces inches apart, warm in spite of the cold.

"We all went to a pub straight after work, everyone from the department, then for a meal and then to a club."

"And?"

"It was good, but I felt... I don't know... really sad, I'd organised the collection and had to give a little speech in the restaurant, it was only me and her who wasn't laughing, in the club we had a few dances and then it was time to go, I'm working tomorrow."

I imagined how he had probably not wanted the night to end, how he had wanted her to grab him touch her fingers to his lips and tell him she had made a mistake, but the fuse of the night had slowly burnt away and the bombshell of leaving had finally gone off.

"I got my coat and she said she had to go too, so we ended up walking through town on our own together, that's why I am soaked."

"Rain."

"Yeah, we rung the taxis and stood together waiting, she said she was sorry she was leaving and I told her I didn't want her to go, we were really close."

"Close?"

"To kissing, our faces were really close."

He shook his head and looked at the palm of his hand; he was holding it inches from his face, seeing her face in its place,

"I can't believe I never kissed her, she was right there, we just stood looking at each other, so close!"

He let out a sigh again and went back to looking at the roof.

"Oh god mate, I feel for you, why didn't you kiss her?"

"I was going to."

"You should have! Why didn't you?"

"You turned up."

Oh no... I'd ruined it; I'd broken the spell as I rolled to a halt. A four wheeled shield that had thwarted Cupids bow.

It was my turn to sigh.

"Oh mate, I'm so sorry."

"It's not your fault, its mine, I left it, eighteen months and I waited till the final second, I'm so stupid."

"Can't you ring her? Send her a text?"

"It's gone now, it's too late."

He sighed and turned back to the window, resigned to a moment that he would remember all his life. A "What if?" ghost that would haunt him whenever he was alone.

A lover's lips never tasted, hair never stroked and hands never held.

Just a moment in a rainy city looking into the eyes of someone you loved.

I can't believe he never kissed her.

14. Funny Old Game.

It wasn't that long ago, after a poor performance in Europe by one of our two great football teams, I got a fare in one of the more leafy areas of the city. It was rather late and drunken and disappointed fans had long since hung up on football phone-ins after moaning about about "poor performances" and "lack of commitment".

I pulled up outside a large detached house and watched as two visions of loveliness headed down the drive in high heels and mini dresses.

They got in the back and asked for a famous Liverpool nightspot and off we went.

"I wanted to stay in tonight I've got university in the morning."

"You've got to come, he told me to bring a mate."

"I've got no money."

"It's okay; he always gives me money anyway."

"Do you think ***** will be there? I hope he doesn't bring his girlfriend, if he is on his own I am going to f**k him tonight, unless ***** is there, I'd sooner do him."

I rolled my eyes and put my foot down, these two were only going to get me down.

When we pulled up at the establishment and as I waited to be paid, I couldn't help but notice that there were an awful lot of gorgeous young ladies standing outside. I watched, as a smart, blacked out windowed Range Rover arrived and ***** got out with someone I assumed to be his girlfriend. The girls outside the car crackled with energy, there were so many pheromones flying around I almost had to put on my wipers. From the back of my car I heard,

"He's brought that f**king slag, how am I going to get him alone?"

And with that, my customers alighted and teetered on impossible high heels, smoothing impossibly tight dresses, towards their rivals and their destiny.

Now, by rights, I should have enjoyed watching them walk away. But to be honest I was profoundly depressed. Depressed that in the twenty first century these intelligent young woman were prepared to be summoned, late at night, to a venue in the city on what can only be described as, a promise.

Jane Austin it wasn't.

I later joked to a friend that they would have to change the newspaper cliché:

"The national grid saying twenty million kettles were switched on at full time."

To

"Twenty million hair straighteners."

It's easy to blame the players, point the finger at the hedonistic young scoundrels bedding all that wilt in their arms. Phallic scythes cutting down all who nurse a glass of champagne before them.

Maybe we should look at the girls, whose lack of self respect and greed distorts their moral compass in such a manner as to make them bed fodder. Willingly succumbing to a liaison that could be the equivalent to a lottery win. Or as in the most recent alleged case, selling themselves for a grand a time... in return for a grand old time.

Or maybe it is us, we who read the headlines, buy the football shirts and subscribe to Sky. It is us who have put these boys on Olympus, should we be surprised if they start to act like gods?

It's also a cruel irony that the man who puts the money in the footballer's pockets, the man who created these Croesus monsters is the one who seems intent of bringing them down. Only thwarted by super injunctions and lawyers, a case of "the media lord giveth, and the media lord taketh away... your celebrity endorsements".

The world moves on, and points of reference change, the days of Dixie Dean eating his fish and chips on the bus home are long gone, and like your tea wrapped up in a newspaper, they aren't coming back.

There is no pink echo, only pink thongs, and maybe we shouldn't be surprised that intelligent, beautiful young woman want to get rich using their skills, they are only looking at young men who did the same.

Besides, it was Jane Austin who wrote in her novel Mansfield Park:

"A large income is the best recipe for happiness I ever heard of."

15. Digital Memory.

I love my mobile phone. Honestly I do. In fact I feel a bit guilty calling it "my mobile phone" as to me it is much more than that.

It has Twitter, so I can tweet from it. Without twitter and my brilliant phone how would people I have never met know:

"I'm about to cut the grass as it's sunny"

And

"Off the pub tonight with the lads, sunburnt after cutting the grass."

And

"Ba ck frum pob, knot tat drunk."

And

"Slept on floor again, woke up by dog licking face in concern"?

As well as twitter it has WIFI, so I can spend my day looking for hotspots to "speed up my connection", walking around holding the phone at arm's length while it searches for somewhere it can call home as I bump into other people doing the same. Joining the masses that walk around stations and cafes looking like an "away team" from an old episode of Star Trek.

Even better than WIFI it has email, enabling me to say things like,

"I just need to check my Emails (always plural)."

And then tut and push the screen and nod and say things like "I'll deal with it later" when I am in company, therefore looking important (If you are doing this be certain to hold the screen in such a manner so as to not reveal you are reading the "Special Offers From Late Rooms, 10% off all weekend breaks" one).

On top of that I can read newspapers on its "HD 3.5 inch capacitive touch technology" screen. I am a news junkie and prior to this phone I could often be found pestering newsagents at six thirty in the morning as they dolefully cut plastic ties from bales of damp pulpy papers that had been outside the shop teasing me since 4.30 am.

"Have you got the magazine as well?"

"I haven't opened them yet."

"I think they are in that pile over there."

"I'll have to go through them all."

"If you could I'd appreciate it."

"Is it this one?"

"No it's the one with the free film."

"This was on the telly last week."

"Yeah but I'm collecting them... I love Dirk Bogarde."

Even better than newspapers (which should be sponsored by Specsavers) I can watch the telly on it. BBC iplayer is a particular favourite, staring at the screen (arms length again, did I mention my eyes are going?) watching telly on my phone is, in my opinion, the best way to watch TV. Well, almost, it's obviously second best to watching it on an actual TV. But it's easier than having an aerial on the roof and a 36inch plasma on the back seat. Okay the screen freezes occasionally and I have to wait for "buffering" (whatever that is), but its great... and it saves me from feeling like I am at work and gives me the impression I am sitting in my living room with a tiny telly and a steering wheel for a coffee table.

And when I talk about my phone I can't fail to mention Facebook! Which is like Twitter but you can ramble, and write "laugh out loud" instead of "LOL".

I used Facebook for things like:

"Hmm looks like a nice day, the grass is a bit long, I think I may venture outside and give it a cut. Don't think I need any sun protection, I live in Liverpool! Who gets sunburnt in Liverpool? Ha ha! I might go the pub tonight...."

This phone is brilliant! It has an MP3 player so I can listen to old songs! And, even better than that, it has a radio so I can listen to radio two playing old songs!

I can text friends about the length of my grass and whether or not they fancy a pint later, and most amazingly of all I can ring my mates and say things like:

"What happened last night? I think I had sunstroke... did I? Oh no... In the middle of the pub? Oh no... I saw the photo on Facebook (on my phone) but it didn't look like me from that angle... just a minute mate I need to check my email....s"

It even tells me the weather and the outside temperature in my current location (in case my windows are painted shut with blackout curtains in place). I swear if I am ever unlucky enough to be taken hostage in the Lebanon and chained to a radiator I hope I've got my phone with me so I can tell if it's raining or not.

The thing I use the most is the camera, it is a "8 mega pixel (count 'em!) dual led flash auto focus" one. And it even takes pictures!

Now when I say use it the most, what I mean by that is I have about 130 pictures of the inside of my pocket (If you ever see someone walking towards you with a "dual

LED flashing" pair of jeans on, stop and say "hello" as it will be me).

I do takes lots of pictures outside of my jeans as well, lots of arms length ones of me (surely the most tragic form of photography ever invented) and lots of one's of empty streets at four in the morning.

I normally take these photos whilst I am waiting for some TV to buffer.

Such is the joy that is my life.

For all the genius of design that the wonderful people who made my sleek stylish HD brushed metal 36GB 2.2 GHz communications device of joy put in... I've some bad news for them.

It's not as good as an old woman's purse.

And the purse in question wasn't a Fendi lamb skinned jewel incrusted gold clasped object of woman's desire either.

It was about six inches long, black leather, a bit tatty with a silver clasp that kept popping open.

This purse belonged to a lady I picked up at a bingo hall one evening. She was a proper old scouser, lots of "Alright lad!" and "I've been playing with our Cissy, she's a miserable cow!" (Names changed to protect Cissy who, being a miserable cow, will probably complain if I she reads this... the miserable cow.)

My old lady had one of those screechy voices only old female scousers have, worn out by years of shouting across tenements for kids to "get in" and calling to their mates across the lines at Meccano or Delco.

We chatted and she told me of her, dead husband, bingo nights and TJ's. Kids living away and "doing very well" the pride of a lonely mother.

Eventually we pulled up at her house and a fat old cat peeked from behind the nets as I told her the fare.

"Ee are lad, you get it out, can't do nothing with this arthritis."

She smiled behind a massive pair of glasses with watery eyes and wrinkled face, passing me her popping purse, holding out her smooth pink hand, dirty yellow wedding and eternity bands hanging onto her finger like rings on a pigeon's leg.

"That's a nice picture."

I remarked of the photo half hidden behind a receipt and a scratched plastic cover; it showed a man, on a beach, sitting on an old fashioned wooden deck chair. He was laughing and was wearing trousers and vest, a little girl was holding a hankie above his head. In the foreground, at the man's pasty white feet, a little boy was importantly digging a hole in the sand, his skinny little arms holding a red plastic spade. He was peering into the hole assessing its depth and wondering if he'd make it to Australia before tea time.

"That's my Charlie, our Alan and that's Dianne."

"It's lovely picture."

"It was taken in Wales... a lovely holiday."

She smiled and looked at the picture at arm's length, as if seeing it through the viewfinder all over again, its colour faded slightly, like her coat and her memories, captured back long before we'd heard of spf and ozone, when summers were long and seaside's thronged and children squinted without sunhats covered in chip fat.

"It's brilliant, captures them so well."

I realised she wasn't listening to me; she was back on that beach all over again, worrying if she'd made enough sandwiches, if the orange juice had enough water in it and whether they had enough money to get the kids ice cream again on the way back to the guest house.

After she had gone to feed the cat, I thought about the phones I've had. How many hundreds of pictures I'd snapped and stored never to see again. Gone are the days of crowding around envelopes and smudging sticky new pictures. We've lost those tangible memories, memories you can hold in your hand, real things that grow old with you, get bent at the corner, and suffer the odd tear, as you suffer the odd tear.

Pieces of paper with names and places on the back in a young woman's handwriting hidden behind a receipt and a scratched bit of plastic.

Biding their time waiting for Alan and Dianne to find them one day.

And then my pocket flashed again.

16. Rag Doll.

I was tired, it was raining, town was packed and I'd just had an argument at a set of traffic lights with a loon who had been banging on my window demanding he be allowed entrance to the warm safe place that was car.

It would be fair to say, I wasn't in the best of moods.

So when I pulled up at the club and a young Amy Winehouse wannabe ran over I didn't exactly perk up.

"Is it fer Rachaellllllll?" she squawked, her massive flower hairclip, looking like a nylon, floral, satellite dish catching my eye; I guessed it was the only flower that smelt of chip fat,

"It is"

"*No wonder the bees are disappearing.*" I thought as I stared at the hair clip, "*there can't be much of a market for chip fat flavoured honey.*"

I decided to try to be optimistic, she'd given me the correct name and I'd only been there for thirty seconds, maybe my night was taking a turn for the better? Besides, I could always turn up the radio if her squawking got too loud in the back.

"I'll get 'err, she's in the bog." Said the flower.

"Hmm... maybe things weren't looking up after all." I thoughts as I watched her waddle drunkenly back to the club.

I put my window back up and tried not to catch the eye of any of the stumbling, shouting, smoking and shambolic throngs that congregate outside certain city centre nightspots at three thirty in the morning.

A few tapped and shouted but I waved them away with a flick of the hand like a Caesar in his sedan chair while I stared, longingly, like a dog waiting at a petrol station, towards the door of the club.

Flower didn't appear.

I finally gave in and took a look around at the passing night. I could see a couple of bouncers demonstrate their best fight moves to each other, dressed all in black, like slightly overweight bald ninjas they threw imaginary overhand rights, followed by lethal kicks to imaginary heads and then rubbed their hands together and winked at the Winehouses who flirted behind menthol Superkings, false nails and blackberry mobile conversations.

Maybe it was time to go home?

Maybe it was time to get a new job?

I glanced back to the club door just in time to see it burst open and watch Flower emerge, like a fire fighter, supporting a limp, bedraggled, stick like, rag doll of a friend towards the cab.

"Great." I said out loud to the air freshener.

I opened the window a couple of inches, the way you do at a hot day in a safari park, not too far, in case the monkeys can reach in.

"She's 'ere."

"Are you sure? What's up with her?"

"She's upset."

"She's not the only one." I said flatly, very flatly.

Amy pulled the door. It was locked.

"Open the door."

"Is she pissed?"

"No! She's just upset!"

"I'm not drunk... honest" The rag doll raised her head, pale faced, blue lipped and red eyed. Her long black hair in rat tails, sticking to wet cheeks.

"Please! She's not drunk, honest!"

I relented; the rag doll looked like she could do with a break. I popped the locks and she fell onto the back seat and quickly pulled the door closed behind her,

"She's going to Widnes," shouted Amy "make sure she gets home!"

"I'm hardly likely to dump her at the side of the road, am I?" Although it had crossed my mind.

"Text me when you get home."

"I haven't got your number." I replied eyeing Rag doll in the mirror, who was scraping wet hair off his face with bitten down fingernails that had barely half a centimetre of black varnish on their tips.

"Not you! Her!" Flower shrieked and I half closed my eyes against the din.

Rag doll smiled at me in the mirror then nodded to flower, at least she'd stopped crying. She wiped her eyes and blew into a tightly packed wad of tissue and we pulled away.

"If you feel sick will you tell me? I don't mind stopping." I said as I passed a fresh McDonalds napkin over my shoulder (I need to get down the gym).

"Honest, I'm not drunk; I've just had a terrible night. Someone just spat in my face and pushed me over in the toilet, they said I was a slag."

"Oh dear."

"They ragged my hair and everything." Her little voice tailed off like she was falling down a well.

"Not the best of nights?"

Rag Doll started to cry again, proper tears with industrial sobs and sniffs squeezing out from behind a damp napkin.

"Hey! You'll be okay! You'll be home soon, nice milky tea then bed, in the morning you'll laugh about this!" I tried to stop them with my best "sympathetic grandma" voice but I don't think she could hear me over the sniffs and sobs.

I rolled my eyes and passed some more napkins over my shoulder (I'm thinking I really, really, *really* need to go the gym).

The sobs got louder and so did the radio. I watched her shoulders jerk up and down; her head bouncing like a Chinese lantern on a rope.

"Oh come on! It can't be that bad." I finally gave in and lowered the radio, worried that I was running out of napkins.

She replied by sobbing some more.

"I'm not really helping here am I?"

Rag Doll shook her head, sniffed and half smiled through that rat tail fringe, her eyes poking out above the crushed up napkins making her look like a really upset outlaw.

"I'm sorry, I don't go out much, first time in years and this happens."

"Why don't you go out much?" I replied, glad she'd stopped sobbing.

"I can't get a baby sitter."

"You've got a baby?" I was shocked; this wasn't empty flattery, she looked like she would need ID to go into Mothercare.

"She's not a baby, she's almost three."

"Three! How old are you?"

"Eighteen, I made a mistake when I was young."

"What do you mean "when"? You still are."

Rag Doll smiled again, this time a little brighter, it almost dried her rat-tails, she was pretty under the thin skin and coloured hair.

"It's the first time I've been out in over a year and this had to happen," another sniff, "I didn't realize his sister would be there."

"Your fella?"

"Me ex fella, he's in prison," Never rains but it pours, "he got eighteen months for slashing some lad."

"Oh dear. So why has his sister got a problem with you?"

"His family said I was a slag, that I tricked him into getting me pregnant."

"I bet the christening was a laugh."

"I didn't have one, there was no one to go, my family don't have anything to do with me either, I moved to Widnes to get away from them all."

"Why Widnes?"

"None of them will travel that far."

I wondered what kind of grandmother thought thirteen miles was too far to travel to love her child and her grandchild?

Thirteen miles, unlucky for some.

"My ex is out soon, he texted me asking could he move in."

"What did you tell him?"

"I said I'd think about it... he battered me when we lived together."

"I hope you remember that, when you tell him he can't move in." Is aid to her via the mirror, this time she didn't smile in reply, she just looked away.

"He's not that bad, he was very sorry, he takes cocaine and it makes him mad."

"He sounds a real catch."

Rag Doll looked at me with sad eyes, lights strobed across her face as we travelled down the motorway, but it didn't brighten her up.

"So how do you cope on your own? Do you have a job?" I changed the subject.

"No, I'm thinking of going to college, but I don't know what to do, I dropped out of school when I was pregnant, so I've got no exams or nothing."

I decided that correcting the double negative wouldn't be the best thing to do considering her circumstances.

"How have you managed to get out tonight?"

"I've saved up for a month, it was my mate's birthday, and the old lady next door is minding Nancy."

Hearing Nancy's name for the first time made me sad, I thought of Nancy in Oliver Twist, corrupted in her youth by her circumstance.

"Nancy is a lovely name, what made you choose that?"

"It was my Nana's name; she died when I was little."

"Have you heard of Oliver Twist?"

"The film?"

I smiled,

"Yeah the film, there was a character in that called Nancy, I remember watching it in my Nan's when I was a kid, one Saturday afternoon. Sitting on the couch with chocolate pudding out of a tin." I decided it was best not to tell her what happened to dear old Nancy.

"I saw that Saw 2 the other day, have you seen it?"

"No, bit violent for me."

"I like horror."

"It's a good job." I thought, as we drove on into the darkness.

17. Decisions Decisions.

"Urgent message for all Delta Patrols to follow, reports of a male carrying a sword on Mill Lane, St Helens, all patrols to avoid the area until armed response have made the scene from West Derby... Delta out"

Les and I looked at each other, mouths open, and then I took up the transmitter for the car radio,

"Delta Control, this is Delta Romeo 27, just to let you know, we are actually sitting on Mill Lane as I speak, do we have a better location for this male?"

As I spoke Les started the car and put his notebook back into his pocket. We'd been sitting catching up on our paperwork after a hectic start to a late shift, it was around three pm and we'd had to dash out of the station barely an hour earlier to a report of neighbours fighting in the street.

"Delta Romeo 27, the male was last seen near to Eaves Lane, it's a bit sketchy at the moment, but we have had numerous calls from residents describing a tall white male, carrying what appears to be a long sword, I'm just getting a message from the incident manager asking 'do you have the male in sight' over?"

We were craning our necks looking up and down Mill Lane but neither of us could see him, I passed this information to the operator who told us to standby while she in turn informed Force Incident Manager, who was normally an Inspector, sitting in the main control room at HQ no doubt nursing a cup of tea.

The FIM's role does what it says on the tin, they pull the strings from afar, until someone of similar rank is on the ground and dealing with whatever it is going down. They are responsible for the Police response, for the safety of the public and the Bobbies on the ground, and like anything in the Police, you got you good ones, and your not so good ones.

"Delta Romeo 27, the FIM is saying you should withdraw immediately from the area. ARV's are en route to deal, received over?"

Me and Les both looked at each other, we knew that there was a primary school less than five hundred yards from where we sat. We also knew that we could turn right and get out of the area in two seconds, or turn left and drive down Mill Lane towards the primary school.

I keyed the radio,

"Does the FIM know there is a primary school letting out shortly?"

"Affirmative, his order stands over."

Right then, at that moment, responsibility had been passed. If we didn't do as we were told whatever happened we would end up in trouble. Les had kids and a wife. I had two cats a dog and a wife... and also a lump the size of a Watney's Party Seven in the pit of my stomach.

"What do you reckon?" said Les.

"We can't just get off" I replied.

"Not really, bit out of order if we do."

"Let's just have a nose then. Okay?"

Les nodded, the buck stopped with us.

We drove towards the school, creeping along we scanned the street ahead. I looked through the wrought iron fence of the playing field as we passed, it flickered like an old film but all I could see was two lonely goalposts and some muddy grass.

"Hang on, what's this?"

I turned to look at whatever Les was pointing out and saw a car coming towards us flashing its lights. We stopped next to the car and Les wound down his window.

"There is a man with a sword down there!" A lady shouted, panicked by the sight.

"How far down love?"

"Just round the corner coming this way!"

"What's he doing? Just walking?"

"Yeah, like he's out for stroll or something!"

"Alright love, leave it with us."

As Les and the lady spoke I was passing on what she was telling us to the radio room. Ronnie, the civilian radio operator was an ex copper with thirty years service. He didn't sound happy.

"Are you aware Delta Romeo 27 what the FIM has instructed?"

"Yeah Ron, but what are we going to do? The school is right here, this place will be crawling with Mums and Dads in a minute."

"Roger Delta Romeo 27. ARV are still en route, I'll pass on the information."

Ronnie understood; he'd been there once.

We drove on, less than a hundred yards away we saw sword guy.

He was tall, well over six foot with shoulders that made him look like a walking door. He had a dirty green military style parka and jeans on with long grey hair, well past those shoulders, and a thick beard that looked like it was eating his face.

His other outstanding feature was the bloody big sword he was carrying.

I felt the car slowing down slightly and glanced at Les, who was wisely buying us some thinking time.

"What do you reckon?" He asked me, without taking his eyes off sword guy.

"Do you reckon it'll be bad form to just run the fucker over?" I replied, only half joking.

Just then, a few doors down behind sword guy, a lady emerged and frantically waved at us while pointing at him. Sword guy turned to look at the lady and then slowly turned to look at us.

"Oh shit." We both said.

Les slowly drove towards him; he was just standing watching us, sword hanging from his massive hand down along his leg.

Les was driving so it fell to me to get out closest to him, if he ran and hacked me to death at least it would give Les a chance to execute plan B... run the fucker over.

I got out and drew my baton, Sword guy was maybe thirty feet away, he lofted his free hand and smiled, at least I think he smiled, all o could see was a flash of teeth somewhere in the thick grey beard.

"Put that fucking sword down now!" I shouted, lifting my baton to my shoulder.

"It's okay." Said sword guy.

I glanced at Les who was still the other side of the car, he had both baton and gas out... covering all the bases in bruises.

"Put that fucking sword down!" I shouted again.

Sword boy took a few steps towards me and I can honestly say that was about as scared I've ever been in my life.

"I swear to god if you don't put that fucking sword down I am going to fucking kill you!"

Behind Sword Guy a few more people had come out of their houses and I noticed an old lady who was standing, hand to her mouth, watching. Somewhere deep inside I felt a bit ashamed for swearing, but this was street fighting Tony, not posh policeman Tony, the apologies would have to come later.

Sword Guy stared at the sword in his hand; I can still remember the look he gave it all these years later. It was like he was seeing it for the first time. He looked from it towards me and then shook his head.

"It's okay!"

"Put it fucking down!"

He took another step and I heard distant sirens, he seemed to hear them too because he glanced up in the air as if they were going to descend on him from above before taking a few more steps towards me.

I decided to do the one thing that you are told never to do when facing an armed person. I decided to advance and crack him over the head as hard as I could.

"Last chance! Put it down now!" I said as I started towards him, I turned side on, both to prevent a smaller target and to give me more of swing with the puny twenty four inches of toughened plastic I intended to fracture his skull with.

He put the sword on the floor.

But I still considered braining him.

"I'm sorry! I didn't mean to scare anyone!" Sword Guy held up his hands.

"Walk towards me!" I slowed as I shouted, I wanted him away from the sword and he did as he was told, hands still raised.

Out of the corner of my eye I saw Les pick up the sword, he must have been circling around us, so he could tackle Sword Guy from the back.

"Kneel down!"

He did, slowly though, his big size had obviously taken its toll on his joints and they creaked under the strain. I realised he was older than he looked, mid sixties maybe even older, he had to lean forward to put both hands on the floor to lower himself down.

We had to link two pairs of handcuffs together to cuff him, he couldn't get his arms around his back, but he looked too strong to risk them to the front. He gabbled incessantly while I tried to talk to him, I was professional police man Tony again now, trying to talk to him down from the emotional heights he'd worked himself up into, but it didn't seem to be getting through.

Sword Guy just kept apologising and telling me he didn't mean any harm.

For all his years, he seemed like a child.

A child with a massive great shiny sword.

It later transpired he suffered from schizophrenia and was being harassed by local kids and that he had gone out to scare them. If I am honest, after chatting to him back at the station, I don't think he ever intended to hurt anyone. He was almost childlike in his reasoning and it made me sad to see him confused and alone sitting in his cell.

The sword turned out to be a 4'6" inch long ornamental one he had bought in an antique shop in

Aldershot years earlier. It wasn't sharp per se, but the tip would have penetrated skin, and a slash would have broken bones and or ripped at your skin.

It had "Excalibur" inscribed down the blade in gothic writing, and when I thought back to the big guy with the flowing grey hair and thick beard striding down the street, that seemed kind of apt.

There is peculiar atmosphere back at the nick after you have had a job like that, Bobbies will stick their head around the door and say "well done", while some will come in the writing room, look at the sword in its evidence bag, and whistle through their teeth and say things like,

"You must be mad."

Or

"I would have been running the other way."

But they don't mean it.

Nearly all of the Police I know live for moments like that, a chance to taste that burst of adrenalin and do something out of the ordinary.

As we sat typing statements our Sergeant came in and sat with us, he told us he would recommend a commendation and that he was proud of us. He lifted the sword in its bag and shook his head then gently placed back on the table,

"I have to say though lads, you must have been sh**ing yourselves when you saw him."

As he was leaving the Armed Response lads came in and they in turn picked up the sword. This time though, one of them decided to try to tell us off,

"Do you know how fast a man with a sword can run at you? That would have gone right through your body armour and out the other side."

"We didn't have any body armour on did we Tony?" said Les.

"I only wear protection in bed." I replied.

"He's talking about nappies." said Les to the ARV guy who was shaking his head.

We weren't laughing the next afternoon when the Superintendent shouted at us in his office,

"You disobeyed a direct order and put yourselves and any colleagues that would have had to come and assist you in danger if he hadn't come quietly! If he'd killed you there is a good chance your families wouldn't have got anything either! You have to think of health and safety, the FIM had risk assessed that job and told you to get out."

"The FIM wasn't there Sir."

"And neither should you have been! Now get out, and don't be playing heroes anymore."

We turned and I opened the door, cheeks burning, angry that I'd just been bollocked for doing my job but not daft enough to start arguing with my boss.

"Oh and lads," we turned, "well done, good job." He said without looking up as he returned to typing on his computer.

All of the above took place in 2002, I have a photocopy of my arrest statement in front of me on my desk right now, I'm proud of that day, and still angry I got a bollocking. I honestly think that 90% of the Bobbies I worked with would have done what we did, not because they were brave, but because it was their duty.

When I joined the job being a copper wasn't about risk assessment forms and health and safety, but it was when I left. I believe the current culture of safety first is there not to protect the people on the ground, be they Paramedics, Firemen or Police; it's there to protect the organisation and their budgets from litigation. Litigation from their employee's and the public. But not only that, the FIM that day, had he told us to go in and had we been chopped up, was individually responsible and potentially liable to a prison term if found negligent under health and safety laws.

So why would he tell us to risk ourselves? He was protecting his own pension as much as the public.

It isn't the emergency services who are solely to blame when they respond in a particular manner to a dangerous situation; it is the lawmakers who have created a society that will attack people who make a mistake in a split second decision made with the best of intentions.

That day in the patrol car, it wasn't a responsibility that was passed to us... it was the buck.

18. Gary's Mum.

"Whoever designed the china tea cup deserves a slap." I thought as I desperately tried to figure out a way to cope with the paper thin one I was currently holding in my big clunky hands.

Index finger too big for the handle, strong tea the temperature of Satan's wee and a coffee table smaller than a box of Swan Vesta lingering coyly just out of reach on four legs that would struggle to hold up a dust mite was only adding to my discomfort. Which, in fairness, wasn't being helped by the arthritic dreadlocked farting spaniel that was resting his head on my leg while trying to focus on my face through milky white eyes that would struggle to see the huge plate of ham sandwiches that balanced inches from his sniffling twitching nose.

The sandwiches, out of all of us, seemed most at ease with themselves. That was probably due to them being together for so long. The ham was so thin it looked like a fissure in the fine white marble of an ancient Greek altar. An ancient Greek altar that had fallen in a vat of cold margarine and then been left in Death Valley for a week.

All this was compounded by an elderly lady trying to suffocate me with fairy cake every time I breathed in. My afternoon visit to a mate's widowed Mum was turning into a trial that David Blaine would shake his head at.

I've known Gary for over twenty years; we met as two spindly teenagers working in a supermarket over the busy Christmas period. On our first day we had both been assigned to work under a vicious old troll of a woman in the wines and spirits department. The old battleaxe would send us up ladders to fetch boxes in the storeroom, always certain to cop a feel as we made our way back down with a box of advocaat balanced nervously on our shoulder,

"Don't worry I'll make sure you don't fall." She'd say as she would grip the back of our nylon overalls with woodbined stubs of fingers as we cried,

"I'm alright thanks!" In nervous falsetto's.

I lasted four days before the beep beep beep of tills and Roy Wood pushed me to the very brink of sanity making me walk out like Captain Oates one lunch time,

"I'll just be some time" I said as I draped my overall over the back of the orange plastic chair I'd been slumped in, for all I know it's still there.

Gary lasted a bit longer; in fact he now manages one of their super duper shiny stores down south. I think the troll ended up being put on trial for war crimes and was hung at the Hague... or at least I hope she was, I like to imagine as she went up the ladder towards the slowly spinning noose the hangman grabbed her bum and said,

"Don't worry, I'll make sure you fall."

"You haven't touched your sandwiches." Said Gary's Mum as she daintily picked the cherry off another fairy cake and passed it to Dog Marley on my knee. "It's lovely to see you Anthony, I don't see many people since the funeral."

I smiled at my full title then frowned at the dog slobbering.

For a moment I felt rather worthy and benevolent for visiting her, the lovely lad who always remembers his old mates widowed Mum, but any thoughts of a Pride of Britain award were quickly dashed in a way only an old lady can with the rejoinder,

"I've not seen you in years."

The lady give'eth and the lady take'eth away.

For a moment even the dog looked disgusted and I swore I saw a sandwich curl its lip at my shabby treatment of an old widow. Guilt flushed my cheeks and I switched the tea cup to my other hand,

"Oh you know what it's like, I'm mad busy, in the cab, writing and all the other stuff, its murder finding the time." Was all I could offer in my pathetic defence,

"It's alright love; I'm only pulling your leg." A gentle nudge from a sparrow's wing of an arm caused me to smile, "Gary says you write a column now?"

"Yeah, for an online magazine, has he not shown you?"

"He has his computer thing, but I don't understand them, takes me all my time to work that." She pointed at a remote control resting on the arm of her chair. Under it laid a TV listings magazine and I could see red circles around programmes of note.

"Do you want me to ask if they need a telly reviewer?"

"I'd be no good, we only really watch the old films don't we Charlie?"

Charlie the dog, raised an eyebrow and broke wind, then went back to staring at the inside of a cataract.

"How old is he now?"

"He's fourteen now, poor old lad is not as fast as he used to be."

I rubbed my hand over the little bony head and he sighed a wheezy sigh, then broke wind again.

It was hard to imagine the bounding bundle of fun that had danced around my feet on a Friday night as I'd waited for Gary to get ready. I looked at the old lady sitting next to me, spindly legs in fluffy pink slippers wrapped in tights so brown they looked like Cuban cigars planted in marshmallows, sky blue cardigan and navy blue skirt, topped with a cumulous of grey hair that was due a set. The same warm face that had opened the door all those years ago was there though, burnished with age but still dashed with the lightest of blusher, applied even though nobody would see it. Not even Charlie.

"I'm glad you've come though son, it's nice to know you still think of me, have another cake"

I didn't have the heart to tell her I'd only called around to borrow Gary's Dad's socket set. I'll pick it up next week when I pop round as promised... as long as I'm not too busy that is.

19. Shuffle tap.

Shuffle tap, shuffle tap, shuffle tap, shuffle tap.

No, I wasn't at my tap dancing class (if you saw me you'd already know I wasn't at a tap dancing class, I've got more left feet than a centipede). I was waiting for an old lady and her Zimmer frame to negotiate the six feet from her front door to my car, shuffle tap, shuffle tap, shuffle tap, tick tock, shuffle tap.

When I'd pulled up at her tiny terraced house in her tiny terraced street she'd been standing at her open front door waiting for me. I'd seen her leaning against the door frame, coat on, carrier bag clutched and, I thought, raring to go. She gave me an arthritic thumbs up and then turned around and disappeared back into the house.

I'm ashamed to say I cursed out loud. You see, a cabbies greatest frustration is someone who looks ready to walk straight out of their front door and then them not doing just that; the turn on the heel back into the darkened hallway will have my eyes rolling long before my wheels.

I peered into the house as best I could and cursed again, just what I needed, a five minute wait while she checked every door and window twice then twice again. I flopped my head back against my headrest and squeezed my tired eyes with my thumbs and forefinger, I'd only been out at work half an hour and I wanted to go home already.

I glanced back at the house then up and down the street while wondering if I'd always been this short tempered or had the job trimmed my tempers length without me noticing, then I heard it...

Shuffle tap, shuffle tap.

I glanced back to the house and she was coming towards me chasing her Zimmer, in one hand hung a carrier bag that was swinging low on her sweet aluminium chariot.

I jumped out, as much to speed things up than to be of service.

"Ee ah love, give us that 'ere, I'll take it." My best scouse for deepest darkest Anfield,

"Oh thank you dear, it's awfully heavy." She passed me the bag, her velvety well spoken voice contrasting with my stereotyping scouse.

I took the bag and placed it on the back seat; before I'd turned she was on the way back into the house, shuffle tap. I leant on the car roof and looked up and down the street again. Many of the houses had corrugated curtains and "Property of Liverpool City Council do not enter" signs on their steel covered front doors. I guessed less than a third were occupied. Liverpool FC's football stadium loomed over one side of the street like a low flying Zeppelin, blocking the sun, in as much the same way as its fans blocked "The Sun".

"One week's wages from a star striker would revitalise this place." I thought, maybe the club didn't want kids kicking a ball outside the ground, just in case the fans stopped to watch them instead of paying forty odd quid you need to get inside the ground.

Shuffle tap, shuffle tap, I turned and out she came again, this time an old sky blue coat with a faux fur collar was helping the Zimmer hold her up. A massive cameo broach sat on her chest like an enamel off switch and a patent leather handbag swung from the frame in place of the carrier bag.

"Can you give that door a good pull for me please?" She asked and I did as I was told. It took me two good tugs before the swollen front door finally filled the frame, I'd thought the front of the housed was going to come down like a Buster Keaton film such was the force required.

"You could do with a plane running over that," I said wondering how she coped,

"It's the damp, it's a good job I don't go out much, once its shut it takes me ten minutes to get it open." She replied as she locked the three locks that also helped to keep her captured.

By the time she'd got into the car and the Zimmer was stowed at least ten minutes had passed from my arrival. I'd given up being impatient; her passage of time had been tougher than mine. I could see her swollen hands and swollen ankles that hinted at her pain, she never complained though, just took her time and thanked me for mine.

As I started the engine and glanced across I noticed her lipstick for the very first time, shiny and red, applied with shaking hand. Her lips looked like rose petals at the end of summer, ready to fall, reedy and dry but with the slightest of memories of what beauty had once been.

"Where to love?"

"The Royal Liverpool Hospital."

"It's full Sunday title?" I smiled, and she nodded primly back in a way that made me feel like she was unaccustomed to making small talk with the "help".

"The Royal" for those of you who do not know, is Liverpool's main central hospital. And if a place bore the title "Royal" that is less regal I for one would not like to see it. A huger cancerous concrete carbuncle you would not wish to see, its tiny windows and towering size are only matched by its greyness.

It seems to suck sunlight out of the sky and repeated attempts to improve its facade have been about as successful as Michael Jacksons were. There is talk of knocking it down and starting again and indeed holes have been dug and clearances has been made, but like a tombstone it stands still, as testament to the short sighted seventies architect who should surely hang his head in shame.

Many passengers speak ill of the Royal, they complain about its inner city drunks who hang around its front doors, begging for change and clogging its wards with their yellow skin and desperate bruised eyes. Some complain of the staff who "don't care" they talk of relatives lying in bed, crying out in pain as if in some modern day Bethel, unseen and unheard or unable to be understood, just one voice in a thousand looking for help.

But many more talk of the "Angels" amongst the staff, who battle against the tide of super strength bugs and super strength alcohol. Angels who "do care", who hold hands, brush hair, sit and talk and fetch sugary tea at a quarter to three for the lost and lonely.

The Royal is like Liverpool itself, trying to change and to undo the crimes of short sighted planners, loved and loathed in equal measures, good, bad and ugly all in one place.

The crinkle of carrier bag brought me back to my car, we were well on our way and my passenger was checking its contents,

"Hope you haven't forgotten anything, I don't think I could get that door open again." I smiled at my lady who smiled back. More relaxed after our silence and some Classic FM.

"There is a trick to getting it open, my husband has it down pat now, he lifts and pushes."

"He must be strong then, I couldn't lift a tea cup after that."

"He was very strong, he's not now, I'm going to see him." She tailed off and so did my bonhomie,

"Oh dear, I'm sorry." I said content to let it drop.

"It's his kidneys, he's had problems for years, it's catching up with him now, he's almost ninety. Been on all sorts of tablets for years, but as you get older... well you know."

"Yeah, I understand." I said, even though I didn't.

"He went in for tests last week, but has taken a turn." She held up the carrier bag, "That's why I am taking him this, I'm sure they aren't feeding him properly, I've made him soup and some rolls."

As proof she showed me the tartan flask, its rusty seams testament to happier times of tea and tides on the beach.

"I'm sure they do feed him, they are very good you know." Was all I could offer, not sure I even believed myself.

"I don't blame them, he's an old man, and they probably don't have the staff to cope, poor things, it's just he is all I have now. And I'm not going to just let him go. I've gone in everyday this week and I think he is looking a little better."

"It'll do him good just seeing you."

"It does me good seeing him." She replied, and I was certain she was right.

I didn't tell her it did me good seeing her, although, as I watched her shuffle tap, shuffle tap, shuffle tap her way through the new atrium doors into the bowels of the Royal, I wished I had.

20. Bye di Bye.

The coarse blanket pushed down on me like a horse hair shroud. I lay on the floor behind the front seats of the car, the heat pawing at my face and sweat trickling through my lank hair and down into my eyes.

"Stop moving." Someone said from above through gritted teeth and I felt a kick and then the weight of a harshly placed boot across my back "You'll give us away."

I heard a match strike and the sulphurous smoke leached through the blanket and pushed what remaining oxygen I had further from my lips.

"I can't breathe!" I whimpered

"Sssh!" Another kick.

My chest heaved and for a moment I thought I might cry, when the smell of cigarettes added to my agony I had to pull the blanket back from my face, I couldn't take anymore. I surfaced like a drowning man, gasping, desperate for sunlight on my face. I looked up, past the occupants of the rear seat and out up to the sky through the back windows, I sucked deep on the smoky air, it wasn't much better than when I was under the blanket. The car lurched forward and then stopped again.

"Get him back under the blanket!" Another kick

"Keep him covered." Another voice, this time from the front.

"If you move again I'll kill you, understand?" Said boots, he flicked his foot again, a physical full stop.

I whimpered.

We'd left home what seemed like hours before, desperate to escape. My father had loaded the car early that morning on his return from the work after a long night shift. He wasn't the only one not to have slept that night, I'd lain awake watching headlamps chase across the ceiling, unable to sleep, excited at what the future held, could it really be true that they gave you free ice cream and that there were brightly coloured places for children to play all day and night? Or was I being teased by my friends? Today was the day I would find out, god willing.

We set off early, deciding to travel in a two car convoy for safety, my father's younger sister, her husband and their children had joined us for the escape. They had the bigger car so my sister travelled with them; they basked in the luxury of rear winding windows and a medium wave radio that they tuned into the state broadcaster.

Nerves were strained in our car, my Mother had the map in front of her as we weaved through the mountain roads, she twisted it like a paper steering wheel as she tried to make sense of our unfamiliar surroundings, pointing at junctions as we passed.

"It was that one! I'm certain! I think." Another cigarette for the nerves, passing it to my father for him to draw on.

"It's straight on, I think." He blinked through the smoke as the tiny engine pulled us up another mountain.

Later she passed me a cup of diluted orange to drink; it was warm and cloying, thick with sugar. The only think it had in common with an orange was its colour, and even that looked unreal. It tasted terrible, but it was all we had to last us, so I drank it, and was thankful.

"Go easy, save some for me!"

I passed the cup to fellow rear seat refugees, my brother, with his boots, and his mate Dave. Dave who shouldn't be there.

We pushed on; nobody wanted to be on these roads at night, I can still remember my father's eyes in the mirror as he watched my uncle frantically flash his headlamps behind us.

"There is something wrong with them, they want us to stop."

My mother strained to turn and look past me out of the rear window,

"What should we do?"

"We can't leave them."

The tick tock of the indicator sounded like a time bomb as we waited for my father to return to the car, we sat on the verge as trucks thundered by until Dad suddenly leant through the window,

"Give me the water, they need it, they are overheating."

"But John! It's all we've got!"

"We can't leave them." Those words again, blood thicker than anti freeze.

What seemed like days later we saw the first signs, our poor car, staggering on like a man in a desert, so close to the oasis.

"Anthony, get on the floor."

"Why?"

"We don't have the right papers."

"But I don't want to go on the floor."

"If you don't get on the floor we can't go in, Dave shouldn't be here." My brother said as he took the blanket from the parcel shelf.

"Why can't Dave go on the floor?"

I didn't get an answer, the blanket went over my head and down I went, trapped in some early form of rendition I felt myself pushed out of sight. My cheek pressed into the carpet as we approached the checkpoint, heart pounding I looked at the springs of the seat in front. Stop, inch, stop, inch, stop.

The window wound down,

"Papers please," click of glove box, "it says there should be a girl?"

"She's in the car behind, they have a radio."

I silently thanked god they hadn't made me wear a frock, suddenly the blanket didn't seem so bad after all.

"She should travel in the car that has her pass."

"I'm sorry, we didn't know, they are a couple of cars behind, they broke down, it's a been a terrible journey."

"Hmm,"

I held my breath; "Please," I prayed, "free ice cream!"

"Okay, straight through the barrier follow the road and don't stop."

We'd done it! The Promised Land! Welcome to Butlins!

That's the most vivid memory I have of the summer of 1978 annual Schumacher holiday, we were having a change from our usual haunt of the much loved Llandudno. My parents had been talked into trying a holiday camp and here we were.

Behind the wire.

I remember the board in the show lounge, "Baby Crying in chalet B4" and I remember "tuts" as some poor mum would have to do the walk of shame on her way to nurse the wailing tot. I remember the paper thin walls and the lino on the floor, and how cold the "heated" outdoor pool was. Kids should have been basted in goose fat prior to immersion.

I recall chicken in a basket and drunken people laughing outside while I tried to sleep, communal singing, bingo and fairground rides with queues that stretched forever.

Even then it felt old fashioned; the colours in the viewfinder looked faded before the pictures were taken.

About two years ago, I did a gig at a holiday camp in Ainsdale. I arrived early, and papers in hand drove up to the gate, the guard waved me in without a glance, this time the barrier was already raised and there wasn't a queue.

I drove through a semi deserted camp that had peeled paint walls and tufts of grass poking through flag stones on the pavement. The fair was silent and a man in an overall sat in a Waltzer reading a newspaper as I drove past, he didn't bother looking up.

I parked at the tiny theatre and looked at the "Coming soon!" board; it read like a lifeboat roster adrift from the seventies that had stopped to pick up some survivors of the early rounds of the X Factor.

I recognized a boy/girl group and a fat old comedian who looked dead behind his smile. Someone was described as a "singing sensation!" I looked at the photo and felt a "stinging sensation!" but at least they had a picture. I was just billed as "comedian TBA".

I didn't even get an exclamation mark.

"Well at least they won't know my name when they boo me off." I thought as I turned away from the poster.

A bright young blue coat was walking towards me, all hair wax and false tan he introduced himself as the entertainments manager.

Manager? He looked so young I was certain my tie was older than him, but I shook his hand and nodded towards the empty camp,

"Doesn't look like we'll be sold out."

"We've got an 80's weekend due in."

I prayed he meant the decade and not the audience average age or I was going to have to spend the next few hours watching Arthur Askey on YouTube for some tips.

"Are you staying for the disco?" Junior asked and I breathed a sigh of relief, pensioners don't do disco... do they?

"No thanks mate, I've got two left feet, and I've left one at home."

He didn't smile; this was looking like it was going to be good gig.

"It gets a bit racy on these special weekends." He gave me a playful nudge and I wondered about that false tan and clutched my bag across my chest.

He led me into the theatre, which looked tired, like it had been up all night partying and needed a good sleep. The stage had a backdrop of silver strips that moved in an unseen draft and I felt like I was back in the seventies and wished I hadn't seen the place in daylight.

It reminded me of Joan Collins with her makeup off, a reminder of beauty past, and best left to the imagination and good lighting.

Junior left me in the dressing room and I sat staring at the bulbs around the mirror that didn't work. Half an hour passed before the door opened a few inches and a young blond bluecoat popped her head round,

"Justin asked me to see if you would like something to eat?"

"Oooh lovely, what have you got?"

"We do a nice chicken in a basket?"

Fresh from 1978.

21. Proper Freezin' Like.

"I'm thick as fuck me, proper thick." She said as she looked over my shoulder at the crossword, "They kicked me out of school when I was thirteen, give up on me, said I was disruption."

"Disruptive?"

"What?"

"Nothing. Did you get expelled?"

"No, I was put on suspension for spitting at a teacher, and I just never went back."

I tapped my pen against my teeth and stared out at the queue outside County Road Post Office, the fact that there was a queue at a Post Office wasn't that unusual, it was the fact that the queue was there at ten past midnight on a rainy Monday morning that made me shake my head slightly in disbelief.

"Are you stuck?" Said my new mate in the back seat, she leant forward again to look at the crossword I'd half finished in the paper on my lap,

"Do you know how much longer your fella is going to be?" I pointed with my pen to a tracky'd up scaly in the queue across the road,

"He won't be long, he's waitin' for his money, it goes in at midnight, don't worry, he'll pay for waiting time."

"I know he will." I replied "What's with the queue at the cash point?"

"Everyone's money goes in at midnight; there is always a queue at this time."

"Rush hour." I muttered to myself, and she didn't hear, or pretended not too.

I'd picked them up at some grimy late sixties flats about half a mile from where we now sat, the sort of flats that always seem to have green mould growing on the outside and propped open ground floor doors with broken intercom panels. They'd come out as soon as I'd pulled up, him striding purposely and her limping behind, his and her track suits and sneers.

I'd been waiting for six minutes now, a cabby's eye on the green digital clock, watching the minutes... and my life, tick away.

"I wish I could do a crossword," she was close to my ear, leaning through the seats, so close I could smell tobacco and greasy hair; she looked over my shoulder and studied the page, "I'm proper thick as fuck."

"That's twice you've said that now, if you keep saying it you will start to believe it."

"I can read and write, can't do no maths though, I hated maths." She sniffed and flopped back into the rear seat,

"I hated maths as well."

"What was you good at? I bet you was good at English 'cos you're doing a crossword."

"I got an o'level in geography." I replied, less than proud but safe in the knowledge I had the edge in academia,

"That was maps and rivers, I hated that."

"You hated a lot about school didn't you?" I moved on from tapping the pen to clicking it.

"I liked history, and art. I was proper good at art, I did a boss painting of David Bowie, they stuck it on the wall in the corridor."

"Do you still paint?"

She laughed a wheezy laugh and coughed a rattly cough as an encore,

"Nah, I don't have time."

I looked across at the queue it was starting to move, Her Majesty's Government had finally got its arse in gear and had flashed the cash.

"Maybe you should go back to college, what would you like to do for a job?"

"I like kids, I'd work with kids, but people like me don't go to college, I like the weed too much."

"All kinds of people go to college, it's not like school it's relaxed, they can help you, I bet you'd get a grant off the dole to go back."

"I'm not on the dole, I'm on the sick, I've got depression and a bad chest, from the weed and stuff."

"Maybe you should pack in smoking it then?"

She nodded silently and looked to the queue herself, her grey face made greyer by the street lights outside.

I was conscious that I was starting to sound like her Dad, so I returned to watching the shuffling line edge forward. It reminded me of those old black and white photos of depression era soup kitchens. Instead of flat caps and overcoats it was black nylon and northface hats. The cash machine was ladling out modern gruel to keep a lost generation alive.

"I've tried packin' it in, but he was doing a bit of dealin' last year so I got back on it." she spoke again, this time sadly looking at me in the mirror.

"Did you feel better when you stopped?"

"Me chest was better, but we moved into that flat and the damp started it off again, so I just started smokin' again. I hate it."

"The weed?"

"Everything." A pause, "All of it."

Her fella was crossing back over the road towards us, waving some cash and smiling like a returning hero from the war.

"Goodison Rd, please lad, I'll be dead quick and then back the flat, what do I owe you so far?"

"It's about eight quid mate."

"Here's a tenner." He said as he placed a damp note on the passenger seat next to me as I drove, I picked it up and slotted it into my wallet, I didn't want to give him time to change his mind.

"Just here mate."

I stopped and he was gone in a flash, darting around a corner like Spring Heeled Jack, out of sight so quickly, that if it wasn't for the tenner in my pocket I'd have never known he'd been there.

"Where's he gone?" I asked.

"To score some weed."

I must have shaken my head, because she limped to his defence,

"He's done really well! He was on heroin and he got himself off that, he doesn't do anything except weed and the ale now, and he hardly even does the ale, he doesn't rob nothing no more, he's proper straight. He got us the flat and loads of stuff for it. The only thing he's got is his weed"

"Fair enough love, who am I to shake my head?"

We sat with the radio between us for a while; I was listening to a report on the cost of tomahawk missiles when she piped up again.

"They shouldn't be wasting money on them, they should be spending money on the likes of us, my back window has been bust for three months now, and they won't fix it."

"Why won't they fix it?"

"He broke it when he lost his keys, they said we're responsible and we should fix it, but we can't afford it, they are bang out of order, it's proper freezin' like."

He came back before I could shake my head again, we set off back to their home and he weighed me in with a couple more quid,

"For waiting lad."

I drove for a mile or two to with the windows open to get the smell of skunk out of the car... proper freezin' like.

22. Mum Knows Best.

She came down the path as fast as her old legs would carry her, waving her arms and shouting,

"Cooheee!"

When she got to the car she banged on the passenger window and I lowered it for the passenger who was staring grimly ahead, pretending he couldn't hear her.

"Here's your taxi fare, you forgot to ask for it!" She said as my passengers face reddened.

"Thanks Mum."

"Did you pick up the bits I bought for you?"

"Yes Mum."

"Make sure you put that chicken straight in the fridge."

"Yes Mum."

"Give me a one ringer when you get home, so I know you are alright."

"Yes Mum."

"Don't use all your credit, I won't pick up till I know it's not you."

"I won't Mum, thanks, we've got to go."

She stood back, wrung her hands like she was trying to split an atom and waved a nervous wave as the window went up.

"Just drive off please mate, she's doing my head in." Said the passenger, who had gone back to staring grimly straight ahead.

"Mum's eh?" I smiled, he didn't smile back. He just shook his forty odd year old head and stuffed the ten pound note into a wallet so empty I almost heard an echo when he shut it.

We drove in silence for a while until he looked into the stuffed carrier back that had sat on his lap like a fat white plastic cat.

"Do you eat fig rolls mate?" He asked without looking up.

"Best not to in this job mate, they make you go the toilet don't they? Or is it the other way around? Best say no, just in case."

"She keeps putting them in the bag because I said I liked them when I was twelve."

"My mum used to do that with those mini chocolate rolls, I bloody hated them but always ended up with a plate full when I went to visit. You should tell her."

He sat back, arms folded across the top of the bag and we returned to silence.

After a while he sighed and said,

"I can't say nothing to her, every week I go round and she's got me a bag of shopping."

Silence again after that.

I glanced across and he was still staring, but now the stares had the glassy look of someone desperately clinging onto tears. I decided to let the radio have a conversation for us and we sat, not speaking for a while until eventually he sniffed and spoke again.

"I lost my job last year, she's brilliant my mum, I shouldn't complain. Don't know what I'd do without her, I feel guilty visiting because there is always a bag by the door when I leave. I don't know how she does it."

"What did you used to do?"

"I managed a warehouse, distribution, been looking for work for nine months now, its doing my head in."

I heard a croak and sniff and saw a sleeve swipe a nose and thought about how hard it must be for a bloke to teeter on the brink with tears in front of a stranger.

But that's what losing a job will do to you, push you over the edge.

Last time I was made redundant I was about 25 years old, I remember Dave, the guy who owned the company, taking me for a walk into the yard, he put his arm around my shoulder and started to tell me times were hard and that takings were down. I nodded and we walked along for a while chatting until he told me,

"We're going to have to let you go."

I replied, with that wonderful stupidity of youth,

"Where?"

"What?"

"Where am I going?"

"The dole son."

"The dole? Why am I going the dole?"

"We're making you redundant."

I still remember the hammer blow, the feeling of it hitting my head then my heart. The thump of it jumping as the words rang home.

I was redundant.

It's a funny word redundant, it makes me think of something that is useless, and I didn't feel useless, I felt young, full of promise and hard work.

Not redundant, not useless.

They let me finish early that afternoon, told me to take the next day off and then work the next week as my last. I got in my car, switched on the engine, drove out the yard and burst into tears. By the time I got to the lights on Picton Road I was pushing out proper big snotty sobs, banging the steering wheel angry with someone but not knowing who.

Before I got home I stopped a while to get my act together, telling myself I'd be okay, a few weeks off and I'd be right as rain, it was going to be a holiday, after all nobody starves in Britain do they?

When I told my Mum she gave me a big hug and told me things would be okay, later on my manager rang me to commiserate and tell me I'd find something quick and not to worry. Even my mates chimed in with back slaps and platitudes about summer days on the dole and new horizons that night when I went to the pub.

I walked home a little drunk and a lot depressed. I'd spent the night laughing off dole jokes and feigning indifference, secretly wanting to burst into tears but maintaining the stiff upper lip.

The house was almost in darkness when I got home, just a lone lamp in the living room guiding me in. Next to the lamp were some little chocolate rolls and a glass of milk. Silently sitting there, like lifeguards at an empty pool, waiting to save me when I fell in.

I hope my unemployed mate enjoyed his fig rolls and remembers... Mum knows best.

23. The Devil And His Mum.

I had a cup of tea with the devil and his Mum the other day. The devil, sitting on a shiny cream and blue leather sofa thanked his Mum when she gave him a plate of biscuits and then blushed when she told him off for not offering one to me first. He awkwardly wafted the plate in my direction and then glanced back at his Mum for approval before popping a whole Jaffa cake into his mouth and smacking his lips.

I took a drink of milky weak coffee from a mug with "# 1 dad" on it and wished I'd asked for tea when the choice had been offered. The devils Mum shook her head at her son who had moved onto to Jaffa cake number three and sipped her own tea from a mug with a faded from the dishwasher Liverpool football club crest.

On the flat screen TV in the corner a couple were looking for a place in the country with a budget that would bail out Greece, or at the very least buy everyone there their own packet of Jaffa cakes and we all silently watched it for a moment until the Devils Mum said,

"If we lived somewhere like that he wouldn't get into the trouble he does."

The devil, by way of reply, ate another Jaffa cake and grunted while shaking his head.

It wasn't the real Devil of course, not unless the Devil wears Homer Simpson slippers and lives in a tidy housing trust property in a slightly down at heel estate in Huyton, just outside Liverpool. This devil was seventeen years old, pale skinned and shaven headed, he had the build of a fly weight boxer and his milky white arms reminded me of a greyhounds legs, skin stretched tight over explosive, long thin muscles laced with quink filled veins.

Where exactly the saturated fat from the Jaffa cakes was going I can only guess.

I'd first met him when I was driving my cab the night before. He'd gotten in with a boisterous mate, both smelling of pocketed skunk weed and chip fat, from an address in the Kensington area of Liverpool and asked to go to Huyton, a suburb about three miles away.

"Been out boys?" I'd asked, by way of ice breaker,

"Sittin' off lad, new fifa on the XBox in'it?" The devils mate had replied, leaning between the front seats to get a look at me.

I turned to look him in the eye and he'd sat back, whatever question he was asking answered.

"Who won?"

"I kicked his arse!" Said the devil.

"Eeee lad, behave," said his mate, "you was shit lad, yer ma would be better than you lad!"

"You couldn't beat me lad, I was playin' as Wigan lad and you still couldn't beat me lad!"

They collapsed in a fit of skunk fuelled laughter behind me and I rolled my eyes as they rolled around.

I should explain, as well as being a cab driver I write, or maybe, I should say, as well as writing I drive a cab. I suppose which order depends on which job has paid for dog food that month. A few weeks earlier I'd been accepted onto The Guardian newspapers Reading The Riots project, the papers attempt, along with the London School Of Economics, to make sense of what had happened on our streets the few short riot riddled days a couple of months earlier. The project involved me interviewing people who had actually rioted on the days in question, sort of "sorting the chaff from the wheat" and sitting down with them to see what they had to say.

I'd found that the leads from The Guardian had proven to be unsuccessful so amongst other tactics I had resorted to asking young people who had got into my cab if they had been there on the nights in question. Most times my questions had been met with stunned silence, with my being acutely aware that I still looked like the Policeman I once was.

This time however my "Do you remember the riots?" gambit resulted in an avalanche of reply.

"Yeah lad, we was there, it was boss, a proper laugh lad!"

"You went to them all the way from Huyton?"

"Yeah lad, we jumped a baxi and got down there to have a go lad, mix it with the bizzies lad, can't miss that lad can yer?"

I laughed along with their infectious excitement and explained why I wanted to know,

"So would we be in the paper lad?"

"No, totally anonymous, there is no way the bizzies can find out about you."

"I'm not arsed if they did lad, would my photo go in?"

"No mate, nobody would know you had spoken to us."

"Do I get dollar lad?"

"No mate."

"Why do it lad?"

"So the government can learn about you, how you live, it might make things better for you, maybe help you get a job."

"I don't want no job lad, they can fuck off lad, they don't care 'bout me, I don't want to help them."

The conversation continued along these lines for a while until I dropped the devils mate off, once left alone with Satan the atmosphere in the car became less charged and he seemed to be coming around to talking to me about the riots,

"I don't want the bizzies to get involved lad, are you sure they won't find out? I'm on a curfew and I don't want banging up again."

I reassured him once again, explaining the highest of journalistic standards would be in place before adding,

"We can meet at McDonalds if you want? So your family don't know." I felt like a potential adulterer,

"Me ma knows I was there, she went off her head, I stunk of smoke when I got in, that's why I only went the first night, I've got a kid, she was going to blow me up to the bizzies if I went again." He said sadly, and I wondered if it was the threat of losing his liberty or losing his child that was making him sad.

"Do you want to meet tomorrow? It'll only take an hour."

"Yeah go 'ed then. About four, come me ma's."

I'd just done a deal with the devil.

In daylight the house looked less run down than it had the day before, his Mum opened the door and shouted upstairs for him to come down when I knocked, she then invited me in an offered me the coffee or tea conundrum I'd failed so miserably.

I took a seat in the living room while she shouted at the ceiling again and a Staffordshire bull terrier wandered out of the kitchen to inspect me and then to loll against me leg,

"Are you okay with dogs?"

"As long as he is okay with me." I replied as he noisily licked two conker like testicles whilst using my leg as support, we both pretended not to notice, me and the mum that is, not the dog, who was concentrating intently.

Mum wandered out into the kitchen and I scratched the dogs belly to distract him from his labours, eventually he slid down my leg and lay on his back accepting my offering of a tickle instead of a testicle.

When the devil walked into the room he looked tired, rubbing a hand across his head his black tracksuit bottoms looked as creased as his grey tee shirt, with his milky white skin he could have stepped out of a black and white film, only Homer smiling up from the floor offered up any colour,

"Alright mate, sorry... I forgot." He said as he flopped down on the couch,

"It was only last night!" I laughed and the devil tapped his head and then shook it,

"He's got a head like a cabbage," said his Mum walking in with my "coffee" and I wondered how much skunk weed it took to help you forget the night before, "He told me about it this morning when he showed me the letter you gave him, how did you find him?"

"He got in my cab."

"You drive a taxi? I thought you were a writer?"

"I am, it's just that I'm rubbish so I drive the cab for food and stuff."

She smiled at my "joke" and went to open the box of Jaffa cakes; the devil sipped some tea and sniffed loudly,

"We still alright with the interview?" I asked and by way of reply he flicked his head to the door and rolled his eyes, I sipped my coffee and we waited for his Mum.

Once she was seated, and biscuits consumption was commenced I asked him again,

"We okay to start then mate?" I nodded to my bag that the devils dog was using as a head rest, "it won't take long."

The devils mum pulled her eyes from the Cotswolds and shook her head at him,

"I don't think he should," she said, and I launched, a little too quickly, into my spiel about sources and safety and society. She listened and nodded and sipped at her drink and waited until I had finished before lighting a cigarette and pointing it at him,

"He's brought me nothing but trouble for ten years, I've had to move because of him, do you see that front door? Twice that's been knocked through by the bizzies because of him. My nerves are shot, you don't know what it is like to have to live with him. His mood swings, his mates, coming in at all hours, drugs, the drink. He's got a baby now... did he tell you?"

I nodded,

"He's supposed to be a father and he couldn't even boil an egg, he hardly sees him, do you?" the devil sighed and looked at the cracks in the ceiling barely listening to the cracks forming in his mother's voice "People like you have no idea." She pointed at me,

"I do! I grew up around here; I work on these streets every night!" I said indignant that I was being seen as a middle class writer type, even though that was what I was aspiring to be.

"I don't mean what it is like to be around here, I mean, you don't know what it is like to be me, what I put up with, what it's like to break your heart every time the Police come knocking looking for him, when the girl he got pregnant comes knocking looking for money, you don't know what it is like! Who is going to interview me? I'm a victim of this too."

The room was filling with smoke from the resting cigarette and we all sat silently for a moment, lost for things to say, the devil stood up and walked to the door, parting through the swirling smoke as he left the room, as the door shut behind him he said two words,

"Fuck off."

So I did.

24. The Sound of Sirens.

Many years ago, in another life, I nervously sat half way down a long table at about ten minutes to ten on a Friday night. Around the table were about fifteen or sixteen Bobbies, two Sergeants and an Inspector.

A St Helens night shift parade, full of experience, intelligence, discipline and me, brand new out of the box straight from training school. Shiny boots and pressed shirt praying to god I didn't make a fool of myself.

I sipped my tea ("we don't have any sugar") was given my nickname (not telling you) and followed my tutor Constable like a collie follows a shepherd.

Later that night I attended my first "B and E now ir ir" (Breaking and Entering Now, instant response, instant response). I can still remember watching the reflection of the blue lights as we passed darkened shop windows, my heart racing almost as fast as the car

"Stick close by, unless you see anyone running, if you see anyone running, run after them... unless they are a jogger...okay?"

"Yeah."

"Just watch everyone, do as they say, okay?"

"Yeah."

"You alright?"

"Yeah! This is what I joined for!"

We arrived at a shuttered row of shops, a couple of other patrols where already there, the two Bobbies at the front stared up at the building, willing it to blink.

"Who's round the back?"

"Jimmy and Bob."

"Come on."

We ducked down the adjacent alley ("watch out for dog s**t"), in one of the yards I could hear hushed voices as unseen hands flicked torches inquiringly across upstairs windows. As I entered the yard I could see a backdoor, its bottom panel kicked through like a missing tooth.

Bob stood waiting at the door,

"Jimmy is inside; do you want to go in?"

"Yeah."

I got on all fours and crawled through,

"Make sure Jimmy doesn't hit you over the head by mistake." Someone said from outside, and I hoped there were joking.

The sound of chuckling followed me in, I shone my torch around and tried to figure out why anyone would want to burgle a butchers shop, I could see lights along a short corridor, Jimmy stood by another broken door, he was glancing up the stairs waiting for someone to mind this possible escape route.

"Stay here, I'm going upstairs."

I did as I was told watching him go, he shouted warnings as he went, skirting the wall and craning his neck to see around the landing. Then I heard a sound that made me physically jump into the air.

The burglar alarm.

At the time I didn't appreciate the significance of arriving before the alarm sounded. It was only a few years later when I noticed that we no longer beat silent alarms, when I say we... by then it was just me. And maybe one other Bobby, who had rushed out off refs to back me up, half eaten sandwiches sitting in an empty canteen waiting for the morning cleaner to tut and throw in the bin.

The days of twenty Coppers bantering around a table had long gone, one night I recall parading with four other Bobbies, an acting Sergeant and the night inspector sitting in an office six miles away battling a mountain of paperwork. On average it was seven or so, paperwork juggling stressed colleagues, moaning about how little sleep we'd had.

That thin blue line was patrolling an area that covered St Helens, Billinge, Rainford, Eccleston, Rainhill, Newton Le Willows and all stops in between, a massive conurbation that made up a third of Merseyside almost..

"Just do your best, and keep an ear out for each other."

Was all the Acting sergeant could say.

I spent longer apologising for being hours late than I did fighting crime. It's difficult to reassure the public when you are dashing out of their front door to back up a colleague,

"Try not to touch anything, I'll be back soon!"

When working day shifts it was a struggle not to wander through a bustling Police station, offices full of intelligence analysts, statisticians, resource managers and equipment officers shaking your head.

I remember chatting to one colleague over lunch. He was injured and due for retirement; he'd been posted to the "Crime Stats Co-ordination" office to recuperate.

"There are almost as many in there than you paraded on nights last week."

He said, somewhat embarrassed, as he nursed his coffee.

I never worked in that office, I'm sure it did an important job, as did the many other deskbound roles in that station and beyond.

What price crime prevention and youth intervention? I'm sure everyone who arrived on a Monday morning at nine o clock could justify their wheelie chair and draws full of marker pens and staplers.

The recent news of the recruitment freezes probably didn't cause many ripples to the men and women who turned out on nights and afternoons this weekend.

The potential loss of thousand of officers through natural wastage wouldn't impact on the Bobby calming down a domestic or searching an empty factory. And the neighbourhood officer facing twenty youths on their own probably isn't worrying too much about budget deficits and estate management costs either.

The "job" has changed; it is constantly changing, civilian managers, hire cars that sit in car parks for days at a time, statistics (and damned lies), diversity, scrutiny and much more now contribute to the war on crime. The recent news that possible use of foreign chiefs from around the world made me shake my, the British bobby, the best in the world, being taught by Uncle Sam, you couldn't make it up.

But if I was getting my head kicked in on a dark street I wouldn't want to hear that "my crime would be recorded in a manner that reflected what had taken place and that its later analysis would enable management to utilize resources in a more appropriate fashion in future."

I'd just want to hear sirens.

25. I Hate Christmas.

I hate Christmas, honestly I really do. I hate the cheery snow covered adverts (let's be honest, have you ever seen people skating with carrier bags outside a department store? They are more likely to go on their arse after slipping on the compacted snow, "Marks and Spencer's don't do broken ankles, Marks and Spencer's do compacted broken ankles with complications of ligament damage.")

If those adverts were realistic they would just show narky blokes pushing trolleys full of bread and milk while their wives said things like,

"Why did our Malcolm have to marry a vegetarian? Do you think she'll eat ham?"

I hate the Christmas telly as well, two hours of watching some cockneys fight in a pub followed by Dawn French dressed as a Vicar makes me want to punch myself in the face. And as for the Queens speech? She should be on Jeremy Kyle not the stamps.

I hate the Christmas parties, every year I invariably end up with groups of people who moan about each other all year long, thrown together in a tight space after consuming too much alcohol purely by dint of the fact they live in close proximity to each other and work in the same building. One by the one they exit the cab, and as they go the remaining ones slag off the one who has just gone,

"He/She is such a cock, did you see the state of their shirt/dress and the way the snogged (insert office juniors or office pensioners name) he/she is old enough to be their dad/mum/daughter/son".

Eventually when I am left with one in the back, I always like to say,

"I'm going to call you for everything when you get out of this cab."

And they will be embarrassed and say something like,

"Oh we are a big happy family normally."

Yeah, the Royal family.

I hate Christmas dinner, not because I have one (I don't, I had spaghetti bolognaise last year out of spite) but because I hate the way everyone invites me around to have mine with them because they think I am depressed on my own (I normally am, but only after watching the cockneys in the pub fighting).

"Come to ours for Christmas dinner, we are only having a few people around." I always imagine myself sitting in the corner while everyone looks at me whispering things like,

"Oh bless, there is only him and the dog, we didn't want him being on his own in case he hangs himself."

Trust me, I've cut down a few people who have hung themselves and if I was going to kill myself that wouldn't be the way to do it. Besides I've only got an extendable dog lead, I'd end up on the landing at the bottom of the loft hatch with a broken ankle and a dog that thought he was going out for a walk.

I hate Christmas crackers, I've had enough disappointing bangs followed by poor jokes at Christmas thank you very much (see above entry re office parties).

I hate Christmas cards, especially ones off the neighbours. I doubt there anything bleaker that a card that says

"Merry Christmas from number 9 to number 4."

It's the kind of thing they used to send Patrick McGooghan to wind him up when he lived in Wales.

I hate Christmas trees, especially when they go up in July (I'm ranting here so that maybe a slight exaggeration). And if you decorate your house with those electric blue lights I hate you. Aside from making your house look like a sun bed shop I keep thinking it's a Police car behind me when I catch a glimpse in my mirror. Stop it, stop it now.

I hate walking the dog on Christmas day, my normally quiet lanes are full of people "having a stroll after lunch" in new hats and gloves. They look at me and say "Out getting a bit of peace and quiet?" and I smile and nod and think to myself,

"No, I'm waiting for my dog to have a shit, like I do every day, idiot."

`All in all, as I mentioned earlier, I hate Christmas.

Last year I worked during the day, (escaping those damn cockneys). It was the usual Christmas fayre, Mum and Dad with the kids. Bin bags of presents and best clothes crammed into the car, Dad's reeking of aftershave he'd unwrapped a few hours before and Mum balancing a pot of something on her lap.

"Remember we can't stay for long, we have to go to my Mum's for four."

"I don't know why we couldn't go to your Mums first."

"We always go to my Mum's for dinner."

"I know, that's what I am saying."

"Just leave it." Through gritted teeth.

Around two o'clock I picked up in West Derby, a couple in their mid sixties, smartly dressed, him grey suit, her best coat. He got in the front, and wished me "Merry Christmas" and told me where to head for.

Once we'd gotten going she asked me if I was working all day and if I had family, now, sometimes I lie at times like that. Sometimes it's easier to create a "normal" life, tell them about my kids getting me up early with their presents and my wife "doing the dinner" and explain that I'm only working for a few hours before I go home for my roast and to put on my new slippers and watch the DVD they bought me.

But this time I didn't, this time I told them the truth,

"No, I'm staying out all day, the dog got pissed at his Christmas party and I'm staying out of his way till he sobers up."

They laughed and I steered them away from the inadequacies of my weird life,

"Are you doing the family thing?"

"Yes, we are going to our Son's and his wife's for dinner, we are running late" he replied, casting a glance to the rear of the car,

"Oh lovely." I said, quickly in case I just started an argument.

"They've had a terrible year, their little boy has been very ill, he's only three and he's has such a tough time."

"Oh dear." I said slowly, sorry I'd asked.

"He's a fighter." she replied

"How is he now?"

"Still fighting." he replied.

And we drove on in silence, thinking of the little warrior and how unfair life could be.

Eventually we pulled up at the house, a modest semi in a nice enough area. The front door was open and daughter in law stood waiting, no doubt alert to the perils of too dry turkey and a Mother in laws raised eyebrow. Holding her leg stood a blond curly haired little boy, he was dressed in a brown corduroy bib and brace, shiny red wellington boots and jumper only a grandma would knit. He watched the car, unsure if it was who he was waiting for, when Grandma got out his face shone. I could spend a lifetime sitting here trying to tell you what it looked like, turn page after page of a thesaurus looking for the word that could catch his smile and tell you how it beamed, but I'd never find one that would tell you how beautiful he was.

His little wellies clumped down the drive as he ran to his nana's arms and when she picked him he was the happiest little boy in the world.

I hate Christmas, honestly I do.

26. Happy New Year?

It had been one of those traditional Christmas's we used to have, you know the sort, wet and raining with grey clouds and warm muggy temperatures of about 7 degrees.

Christmas day had slid into Christmas past, all that was left to remember it was a few glimpses of ripped wrapping paper when you opened the bin and that stain on the carpet where someone kicked a glass of wine over,

"Why did you leave it there?"

"Open your eyes!"

"Get a cloth that'll stain!"

"I told you we should have got the brown carpet!"

"Pour salt on it."

"We've only got those little ones we pinched from KFC, I've got vinegar?"

"It's a carpet not a bag of chips!"

The world had limped back to work for a few days rubbing its forehead and moaning about "going abroad next year". All around buses full of mumbles about "his mother ruined it" and carpets being ruined.

Bank Holidays had blurred into the normal seven day rota of the taxi drivers calendar, I was glad that I no longer had to listen to Slade and that Shane McGowan had earned enough money to cover his bar bill for another year, only one more night of madness to go... New Years Eve.

The more astute amongst you may have noticed, after my last column, that I am not particularly fond of Christmas and its glistening balls of doom. But please, standby, I am about to go out on a limb... I quite like New Years Eve.

Let me tell you why.

Many years ago, as a boy I spent a Saturday Night watching The Outlaw Josie Wales on BBC one. I'd had a long day at the office fighting Indians and Nazis and as I sat on the couch with a slice of Madeira cake my final battle was one with tiredness. But I loved westerns and it was Saturday so my Mum turned a blind eye and I saddled up with Clint (in my pyjamas) and off we rode to avenge our way through Missouri and beyond.

Some may recall on his mission he was accompanied by an old Cherokee Chief, they meet for the first time at the end of Clint's pistol (steady ladies).

The Indian is embarrassed that he's let a white man sneak up on him, and to hide his shame he tells a story, it's a wonderful moving moment played to perfection by Chief Dan George. But as a boy it wasn't just the story that entranced me, there was also a line of dialogue that jumped out of that old Indians speech that made our D.E.R. 20" rental television larger than if I was watching it on IMAX.

"We must endeavour to persevere."

When I sat down to write this piece that line popped into my head because my Mum once repeated it back to me down a crackly phone line one New Years Eve many years ago.

I was standing in a phone booth St Thomas, a little worse for wear after drinking all day at the beach with some friends before we went back to the cruise ship we worked on. It had been a glorious day but at the back of my mind I remembered that my Mum was facing another new years eve without the love of her life in a lonely old house with nothing but the Daily Mail TV guide, a glass of snowball and Stanley Baxter for company.

"Why don't you go to Denise's or Phillips for the night?"

"I don't want to bother them."

"They are your son and daughter for god's sake! They won't mind!"

"No, I'm going to watch the telly, have a snowball and go to bed, I'll be okay, anyway what's your new year's resolution?" she said, changing the subject in that way that mums do when they don't want you to worry.

"To buy some alka-seltzer, I'm going to a party tonight, what's yours?"

"To endeavour to persevere."

We laughed at our private joke. I'd told her about that line and its impact a couple of years before, when she'd fell apart after my Dad had died and we had sat talking in her room one night. She had understood that it didn't mean to improve; it didn't mean to change your life, win a gold medal or find a cure for cancer.

It just meant you would keep trying to keep going.

When she was very ill, years later, lying in bed, with tubes up her nose and a machine that bleeped every time she breathed, just to remind her she was alive, she'd whispered it to me again,

"Endeavour to persevere."

And she did. She made it through New Year into the new millennium, and I was proud of her for doing so.

Years passed since that machine stopped bleeping, and I travelled many miles by many means. But the new year this story relates too took place in my taxi and played out over just two at the most.

It was about ten to twelve, I sat in the car waiting for the post midnight rush, girding my loins for the countless "All the bests" I'd have to hear when out of the blue I got a job.

I was surprised, who goes anywhere at midnight on New Year's Eve? If you aren't kissing or shaking you are texting. No one is travelling, not even the taxi drivers. I pulled up at the tiny terraced house in Bootle, and an old lady came out and sat in the passenger seat next to me.

I've written in my pad that her coat smelt of damp wool, like a sheep in a shower, and that she was wearing a headscarf that was sky blue and almost see through, the kind don't see any more.

She clutched a bank card and asked me to take her the cash point and off we set through the silent shiny streets of Bootle. The rain had stopped falling and the year was inching to a close as I waited for her to draw whatever cash she needed. She entered her numbers with the slow deliberate taps of a pensioner and eventually returned to the car with a ten pound note clutched in her hand.

"Back to mine please lad."

And off we set; she fended my conversation with a couple of nods and a shake of her head so the journey was mostly silent except for Big Ben giving it large on Radio Four.

"Happy new year."

"Same to you lad."

"That's five fifty please love."

"Keep the change."

And she was gone.

I looked at the tenner and her fast closing front door; she hadn't wanted to spend that New Year on her own.

Happy New Year everyone, and please, spare a thought and raise a glass for those who are endeavouring to persevere.

27. My BFF

A friend asked me this week "How many friends do you have?", well, I say a friend asked me, I've never met her or heard her voice, for that matter I don't even know what she looks like. And when I say she asked me, what I actually mean is she tweeted me and the three hundred other people she "knows" on twitter.

We've had a few decent conversations in the past; obviously they have been limited to 140 characters or less, that and whether or not T-Mobile have turned the coat hanger they have for a mast near to where I live around to face my house, but other than that I think it's fair to say she is a friend, even though we'll never meet or actually converse face to face.

Thinking about it... for all I know she is a fat bloke in Wigan.

The whole friendship thing popped into my head again today when I was walking the dog, coming towards us was a lady I say hello to pretty much every day of the week. She takes her Jack Russell out at about the same time as I take the flea bag I live with, and our paths (and leads) cross on the main road close to where I live. We normally stop for a moment, to allow for the sniffing of bums (the dogs that is) and to discuss the weather whilst ignoring the canine snorting ceremony in a terribly English way, fifteen seconds later we move on with a "Cheerio" and a "ta ra" (she's posher than me).

Today as we chatted about drizzle, her mobile rung and she answered with,

"I'm just chatting to a friend, I'll call you back"

I almost looked over my shoulder for her friend, then I realised she was talking about me. I don't even know her name and she called me her friend. We concluded our discourse "Better get on, I've got dancing tonight" she said and then waltzed off.

I carried on walking pondering my new found "friendship" and the value of what we call a "friend". I thought about my best friend, he lives in London; we met on the first day of infant school in 1972 and we pretty much sat next each other in school right up to leaving in 1983 (except for one year that he won't let me forget, when I was stuck in the thick class because the teachers couldn't read my handwriting (not because I was thick, honest)). We travelled the world together working on cruise ships; Greyhound bused around the USA twice and once lived on a hotel roof at Miami airport for six days because we had no money. We normally chat a couple of times a day about nothing, he winds me up and I wind him up, when we meet we've been compared to a pair of old ladies bickering.

I love him, although I'd never tell him, because he is a fat idiot who gets on my nerves, and besides, just to confuse matters further, he isn't a friend he's a mate.

Now a mate is a sub division of friend, in many parts of the UK it would be considered to be lower down the pecking order than friend. But in Liverpool a "mate" is better than a "friend"; you would never hear a drunk with his arm around another bloke's neck saying

"You're my best friend you are, I love you I do"

For that sort of drunken sentimentality only "mate" will suffice.

A mate will tell you things a friend will never do,

"he/she was never good enough for you"

"you've got bog roll stuck to your foot"

"There is a lump of food on the edge of your mouth"

Think about it, if it wasn't for our mates we'd all be walking around with bits of cornflake on our chin whilst the rest of the world pretended it wasn't there.

A couple of months ago two young female friends got in the cab as my hectic Saturday night shift was coming to an end. My heart sank as the bleached blond beached on the back seat and started to sob in a way only a forlorn drunk can do.

"Waaaaa haaaa haaa ha! Waaaaaaaaaa ha ha ha" she replied when I asked where we were heading,

"Maghull mate" replied her mate as she smoothed her friend's fringe from her sodden face

"Waaaaaa haaaa haa ha" said chuckles as I hired the radio and tried to bend the steering wheel,

"Is she okay love?"

"She's just caught her dick head fella kissing the face off some girl"

"Waaaaaaa haaaaaa haaaaaa" said her mate in agreement, head bobbing like an Iron Maiden fan during an encore.

"He's not worth it love" I said over my shoulder "There's plenty more fish in the sea" I was now aware that I was starting to sound like I was reading from a book of "Cabby's Consoling Clichés" so I decided to shut up and leave them to it.

"Come here" said her mate and pulled blondy close, putting her arm around her and wiping her cheeks with a tissue. The gut wrenching cries of anguish abated to softer intermittent sobs and she rested her head in her mates lap and I breathed a sigh of relief I wasn't going to have to listen to her all the way to Maghull.

I lost myself in late night radio and route planning as we ambled on our way; it was only after a few miles I realised I could hear the sound of chuckling coming from over my shoulder. I watched the mirror as Blondy's mate whispered in her ear and smiled as Blondy giggled through the tears and nodded her head.

After a moment Blondy turned and said "I love you, thank you for making me smile" and they hugged and then sat in silence, friends forever, there for each other, sharing a the sort of love that doesn't need a valentines card, or an overpriced rose from a Chinese lady in a pub.

The sort of love that comes only with friendship, not the love that was nurtured in the marketing department in a greeting cards company, the love that was nurtured over time with warmth and trust.

I might phone that fat idiot in London in a minute, maybe you should phone yours too.

28. The Scene.

The back of my neck was soaking, my feet were soaking, the back of my legs were soaking (but that was okay because it meant they matched the front and the sides), my forehead was soaking and I'd taken my gloves off because they were making my hands soaking, soaking and a weird shade of blue.

I was wet, wet with blue hands.

The reason I was wet was due to the fact that I had been standing in the pouring rain, bereft of shelter, for about four hours. I'd reached the point where I didn't want to move because it made my thick woollen trousers rub against my legs which caused me to shiver, which made me move, which caused... well you get the idea.

Let's just say I was wet. Wet and cold with blue hands.

The day had started out well, it was my first day back from some much needed leave, the sun had been shining as I'd gotten into my car and drove to work and I was in the mood for some serious policing, or at the very least some light hearted policing. On the way up to the Constables parade room I met the station equipment officer who threw me a wrapped pair of new gloves,

"Don't lose these ones!"

"I didn't lose my last pair, they got covered in blood and I threw them away."

"Well just remember, these cost money and they don't grow on trees."

"I know they don't grow on trees, its mugs that grow on tree Dave."

He ignored me, no doubt still bristling from having to give some equipment to someone.

It's a curious thing in the Police that the person whose job it is to give you stuff hates giving you stuff. Every equipment office I ever met treats their store room like it's their last Rolo, they guard it like some sort of Norse Troll, ready to fight to the death for the last piece of Photocopy paper.

"What are you doing with all of these batteries?" One once asked,

"I'm putting them in my torch."

"Do you have to use it so much?"

"Only of a night."

"These cost a fortune."

"Maybe you should give us carrots to help our night vision."

"I'm not made of money you know."

My attempts at trying to explain it wasn't actually his money fell on deaf ears, although in fairness, he probably didn't have any batteries for his hearing aid.

I was unwrapping the gloves as I walked into the parade room, Bob Osborne was typing at a computer near the door, and he glanced up as I passed,

"New gloves?"

"You should be in CID Bob." I said as I walked to the parade table, and took my usual seat.

The parade table in the Constables writing room at St Helens could easily seat in excess of twenty Bobbies. It was a long thin series of six foot tables locked together with uncomfortable orange plastic chairs scattered around. When I walked in on my first morning back from four days rest there were two coppers huddled at its tip making it look like one of those massive charity thermometers, except this one was collecting coppers, and by the looks of it, they weren't doing well with the appeal.

"Is this it?" I asked as I took my place opposite Sungy and his new sprog,

"We won't need any more, now you are here." Phil Sung didn't look up from the notebook he was writing in, his probationer smiled nervously and checked her pens and tried not to be noticed,

"Alright mate I'm Tony, I'll introduce myself seeing as he wont." I said holding my hand out.

"I'm only bothering to introduce her to people that matter," Muttered Sungy, "obviously you wouldn't be on that list."

"I'm Kate." said the sprog, shaking my hand.

"When you have finished working with him, give me a shout and I'll show you how to be a proper bobby." I replied.

"You should wash that hand." Said Sungy, looking at Kate, "He has some terrible habits." He returned to his notebook, ignoring the pen I'd thrown at him.

The Sarge wandered in with a pile of paperwork and a pained expression. He took his seat and Bob wandered over and sat next to me,

"Alright Shoey, good holiday?"

"Lovely Sarge."

"New gloves?"

"I've had the old ones re-sprayed."

"They look like new." He replied sighing and shifting in his chair whilst pulling a face.

"You okay Sarge?" said Bob.

"It's my knee," said the Sarge, "It's killing me."

Sungy glanced at me and smiled and I stared at the table and tried not to laugh.

The Sarge's knee was a cause of much hilarity on the block, his constant pained expression and theatrical squeezing always raised a smile, one colleague had started referring to it as "alladins lamp" due to the amount of rubbing it received.

I tended not to comment on it, the fact was the Sarge didn't like me, and I wasn't overly keen on him, so I'd decided not to give him more reasons to hate me than he already apparently had.

"Don't get comfy Shoey; I need you to mind a scene."

See what I mean?

Being told to mind a scene in the Police is the lowest of the low, don't get me wrong, it's an important job, whole cases can collapse on a badly preserved scene, but once the goose has flown its basically an admin job that a monkey with a watch and a pen could do. In those days if there were no monkeys with pens around the job used to be given to anyone who couldn't drive or was useless. Nowadays it is given to a community support officer. Which means the monkeys with pens can get on with proper work.

"Why am I minding the scene?"

"Because Sungy has his sprog, Bob is up to his eyes in paperwork and there is no one else to do it."

"What about Neighbourhood can't they do it?"

"They've had it all over the weekend and they are short today, it's only till twelve, one of the afternoon shift is coming in early to cover from then, Sungy will run you out there after parade so the night lad can go home."

"Run me out? Why can't I take a car?"

"We haven't got a spare for you, you'll have to stand outside, it'll do you good to get a bit of fresh air." He replied, not looking at me as he sifted through paperwork, his mind made up.

I looked out the window at the blue sky, it was January but the weather had been quite mild during my holiday, I consoled myself that it might not be too bad after all, a nice morning chatting to locals about the weather could be a relaxed way to ease myself back into work.

"Where is the scene?" I asked.

"Concrete city." Sungy replied smiling.

"Oh god." I replied, not smiling.

"Concrete city" was the name given by the locals to a massive council estate on the far side of St Helens, it had been thrown up by the corporation to house the masses after a slum clearance and it fitted every stereotype of poor planning you could think of. No shops, dark alleyways, no buses, bikes with no wheels lying in the road like carcasses on a tarmac Serengeti with gangs of kids hanging around them after nightfall like hyenas, nothing to do and nowhere to go.

I was often tasked to work there on response (I told you the Sarge loved me) in the Delta Romeo 27 car, and whenever I was I knew it would be a long night of domestics, violence and disorder. The place sucked the life out of me, pretty much the way it sucked the life out of those who lived there.

"You'd better get going, Sungy will give you a lift." Said the Sarge and as I sighed and stood he held up a pile of files, "When you get back I've got some paper work for you to sort as well."

Deep joy and so much for light hearted policing.

Down in the locker room Sungy sat on the step watching me get my kit ready for the morning, although we moaned about each other incessantly we'd been mates for years, having joined the block only weeks apart as new Bobbies. Now Sungy was a trainer Constable, entrusted to nurture fledgling careers, it gave him the pick of jobs on the system, but with that perk also came the burden of never knowing who his new partner was going to be, or if he'd have to recommend that they be binned from the job, for a genuinely nice guy that was always a major worry for him to deal with,

"How's it been since I went on holiday?" I asked.

"Crap."

"How's your new sprog?"

"Crap."

"What do you reckon the weather will be like today?"

"Crap."

"It was sunny before, what is the forecast."

"Crap." Said Sungy as he stood up and walked towards the exit of the locker room.

"Where are you going?"

"Crap."

I shook my head and stared into my locker weighing up the pros and cons of taking my waterproof trousers and decided against it. This was in the days before breathable waterproof fabrics, back then waterproof meant heavy and sweaty. And previous experience told me that "being relieved at midday" usually meant standing around till two thirty pm, with aching feet and a full bladder so I didn't want to add sweaty legs and rubber trousers to that equation.

I wasn't incontinent.

"If I give you my waterproof trousers will you drop them off to me if it starts to rain?" I shouted.

"Yeah whatever." Replied Sungy from behind a distant cubicle door.

"Are you alright?"

"Just fed up waiting for you to sort out your winter wardrobe." Like I said... we were great mates.

I grabbed the trousers, belt kit, baton, gas, body armour, big hat (custodian helmet), clipboard and pens, so much for travelling light.

"Welcome back from your holidays." I thought.

The drive over to the scene was spent mostly listening to Sungy complain about his "guts", a constant diet of take away Fried Chicken since his divorce was taking its toll not just on Phil but the rest of us as well.

"Have you tried cooking for yourself?"

"I never have time."

"If you've got time to sit in the drive through, you've got time to cook in the kitchen."

"Yeah, but it's not just cooking is it? I've got to buy the stuff, then cook it, then eat it and then do the dishes, I never have time."

"You can't just carry on eating chicken Phil; you are going to get scurvy!" I said marvelling at how lazy a man could actually be,

"I don't just eat the chicken; I get sweet corn and gravy some times as well." He said rubbing his stomach and pulling a face.

"Well as long as it's a balanced diet." I replied, watching as he popped another ant-acid mint into his mouth and broke wind violently.

We arrived at the scene I found a tired night shift Bobby sitting on the garden wall of a late sixties terraced council house. It looked like it had been gift wrapped in the blue and white crime scene tape that fluttered in the morning breeze.

He thrust a tattered red clip board in my direction,

"It's all yours; I've signed it over already."

I opened the folder and halfway down a creased crime scene log saw his name and collar number next to the time, he watched me sign my name next to his and then collected his dew covered belongings from behind the wall.

"What's the story with the job?" I asked as he folded a copy of the daily mirror into his coat pocket.

"Some old alkey took a tumble down the stairs and managed to break his neck."

"Is he dead?"

"Guessing by the way he'd been lying there for a fortnight I think so, they got the dates from the post under his head and compared it to the dates on top of his head."

"An unknown mail deceased?" Judging at my night colleague's lack of smile I guessed he was tired and needed his bed. Either that or it was a terrible joke... he must have been tired.

"What's the score around the back? Is it secure?" I asked before he went.

"Boarded up, you've only got the front to watch. They reckon they will release the scene in a couple of hours." He replied, his voice heavy with lack of sleep and lack of enthusiasm,

"Here's hoping."

The night Bobby nodded wearily and trudged across towards Phil who was waiting in the warmth of the car.

"Are there any friendly locals?" I asked tipping an imaginary cup of tea to my lips.

"Around here?" Was all he said as he threw his kit on the back seat, "What do you think?"

"Can I have the newspaper?"

"I'm still doing the crossword."

"In your pocket?"

"When I go to bed." He said as he slammed the door.

I watched as Phil gave me two fingers as the car pulled away and the night bobby opened the window, no doubt because of the "fowl" smell.

Looking around at the early morning street once they had gone, every house looked pretty much the same, except for the odd expression of individualism that manifested itself via concrete pineapples on gates posts or depressed looking metal butterflies on a wall.

When I think back to concrete city I think the thing that got me down the most was the lack of grass and trees. It was like the builders hadn't wanted to hang around at the end of throwing it up and had decided it was would be quicker to just pave the entire area. Outside of the tiny front gardens of the houses the only green to be seen was on the dirty weeds that clung to life in the cracks between the flag stones. In summer they would have tiny yellow flowers that reminded me of alpine blossom clinging to life at ten thousand feet, except these flowers had it much tougher than their Bavarian cousins. They battled being stood on, kicked and forgotten, a bit like the people they lived alongside.

I noticed an old guy coming out of his house a few doors down, he closed his rickety front gate and limped in my direction, his heavy woollen overcoat failing to disguise his bent back and withered body.

"Morning!" I smiled as he walked past me on his way to the row of shuttered shops some five hundred metres away,

He nodded but didn't speak; no doubt off to get his morning paper from the distant shops before they became the sticky sweet that attracted the waspish kids on the estate. I was always amazed when working nights how early old people of rough estates get up and go for the newspaper. I used to blame it on errant prostrates until one once told me,

"It's the only time I feel safe, when they are all in bed."

"They" being the teenagers, "They" being someone else's grandchildren.

I sat on the wall and flicked through the incident log; the scene was two days old and had been started by the first Bobby to find the old guy who'd died. I looked through it and watched an investigation unfurl, thrive and then wither. Bobby, Doctor, supervisor, Duty CID, CID Supervisor, Soco (back when they weren't named after an American TV series and wore trendy jumpsuits) Undertakers, CID Inspector, and then a long list of beat coppers left to watch over the scene like a little dog at his masters grave waiting to put out of his misery.

As I read the log a fat blob of rain spattered onto the page and magnified everything under it, I wiped it away and looked into the sky; some grey clouds had snuck up while I wasn't looking. I looked down at the smudge on the paper and closed the folder and slipped it into a plastic bag I always carried in my pocket. By the time I'd made it water tight several other blobs of rain had come to look for their mate and by the looks of it they were calling for reinforcements in the search. The street was noticeably darker and down by the shops I could see my new pal trudging towards me, bread and newspaper clutched to his chest like a newborn.

"Nice day for it." I said as he passed, a watered down joke if ever there was one.

He didn't reply, just looked at me in a way that said "I've been getting pissed on all my life, why today should be any different?" And carried on to his house. I noticed how he hadn't walked any faster in the rain than he had when it was sunny. Maybe he was going flat out.

The rain carried on coming, hour after hour. I listened to my radio chirp occasionally to remind myself I wasn't the only person left on earth, and that, plus the odd passing car splashing past kept me company. My waterproof coat had long since admitted to being a liar, my back and shoulders where soaked, I could feel every fibre in my thick woollen jumper through my shirt and I was dreading the moment when I'd have to move. Even my helmet was leaking; it felt like a sodden crown of thorns digging into my brow and weighed like a bag of sand balanced on my head. My trousers were wetter than a sharks eyeball, as were my feet, in fact, the only thing that cheered me up slightly was the fact that I couldn't feel them anymore.

At least I had my new gloves to keep my hands warm, except they didn't. They were soaked and too tight. All in all, I was feeling a bit grim when a scruffy red Ford Fiesta pulled up in front of me and the window wound down an inch. DCI Ronnie Conroy looked out and smiled, like a man hiding in a heated letterbox.

"Alright Shoey?"

"I'm almost drowning boss but other than that I'm great."

"I'm still trying to clear the scene, as soon as I get the nod I'll let you go."

"Any idea how long boss?"

"Not long now."

I shuddered, not just through the cold, but because "not long now" was the Bobbies prayer, and it was a prayer that was seldom answered.

"Do you want a brew Shoey? There is a cafe down at the shops, I'll get you one."

"Oh boss that would be fantastic."

He gave me the thumbs up and revved the little engine and headed off, Ronnie Conroy, my saviour. I watched as he pulled up at the shops wondering if he'd push the boat out and get me a bacon butty. The red brake lights shone through the rain for a moment, and I watched as they went out and the car performed a swift U turn and headed back towards me, as he drove past he held up his radio and shrugged. He'd been called to another job, my heart, like my morale, plunged to new depths and the rain seemed a tiny bit heavier on my shoulders.

I took a glove off to wipe the water from my face, as I lifted my hand I noticed it was blue. Not a "just read the papers" blue, it was a "dipped my hand in some blue dye" blue. I stared at it and then wiped it on my coat and rubbed it with my other hand, it was still blue, very blue.

New glove blue.

I swore loudly and rubbed it again, this time on my trousers in the hope the thick wet wool would scrub it off, it didn't.

"You alright mate?"

I turned, three teenage lads had wandered up behind me, dressed in tracksuits and trainers they were oblivious to the rain, shaved heads glistening with an air of pester the copper they stood before me,

"No, I'm drowning." I replied as one sat on the wall, testing both its and my strength "Don't sit on the wall mate, it's a crime scene."

"I'm only sitting on the wall."

"And I'm only telling you not too."

He hopped down and kicked an imaginary stone while his mate spat an imaginary spit.

"What happened here?" Said the tallest, looking at the house.

"Old fella died, did you know him?"

"It weren't nothing to do with us!" Said the sitter, indignant at the perceived accusation I hadn't made.

"Alright calm down, I never said it was, I was only asking if you knew him?"

"He was on old miserable bastard, lived there for years, always moaning 'bout us." Said the tall one, looking at the house remembering confiscated footballs galore.

"Well he won't be moaning anymore." I replied and we all nodded, united for once in the realisation that death, when it got you, tended to get you good.

The lads wandered off with a few mumbles and I watched them go, sloping off to nowhere to do nothing, a life full of negatives.

God I needed to get out of this rain.

It was another hour till the tall one reappeared; he had that ninja thing down really well because it wasn't until he put the mug on the wall that I knew he was there.

"Me mam made you a cup of tea, and there's some biscuits." He said as I turned around.

The steaming mug and chocolate biscuits lay between us like a peace pipe in a western; I pulled off my gloves and grabbed the mug, enjoying its warmth burning my skin.

"What's up with your hands?" Said my new mate.

"New gloves." I replied.

29. Sudden Pudden.

Coppers call it being "fresh off the shelf", I was a straight out of training school bobby with my tutor Constable driving on a freezing St Helens morning to a report of a drunk lying in a communal garden asleep,

"It's a bit cold to be having a kip in a garden."

My tutor Gary glanced across and smiled at my ignorance,

"The radio op said he's been there for two hours and that the lady who reported it had been shouting him for five minutes before she rung, I don't think he's asleep Shoey."

I nodded and tried to act nonchalant whilst inside my stomach did a little flip. This looked like being my first sudden death report. The more experienced Bobbies called them "sudden pudding" and we new recruits tried to affect their casual tone when we talked of them amongst ourselves. We knew that our first one was coming, it was inevitable, most of us wanted to get it over with, face the fear and push through it, I was happy to wait as long as I could. An old Bobby in the canteen had shook his head and said,

"You've got thirty years of them, the longer you don't have one, the less there'll be in the long run." And I

while I was happy to put it off, it was starting to nag that I'd still not had to look one in the face.

I'd only joined fourteen weeks before that day, I'd come to the "the job" relatively late at the "mature" age of 27. Prior to be becoming a bobby I'd tried all sorts of different careers, ranging from roofing to selling jewellery on cruise ships, but none of them had fitted me. I always seemed to get bored and move on, looking for new challenges and excitement.

When my fiancé told me she had seen the ad for the Police I'd initially dismissed it as a waste of time applying, we'd recently returned to the UK after having worked in the Med onboard an Italian cruise ship, unemployed with a mortgage and a wedding to pay for I'd found work managing a builders yard and I hated it. Hated it with a passion.

"I'll not stick it, besides; do you really see me as a copper? I'm not exactly cut out for the role."

I'd grown up in a tough working class area of Liverpool, there were no Police in my family, in fact, there were no Police in my postcode, but I didn't have a criminal record, I was relatively fit and able and blessed with a quick wit and a nagging wife to be. So, I gave in and applied. Every few weeks there was another stage of the application, fitness test, pass, intelligence test, pass, initial interview, pass, group interview, pass and then, joy of joys, letter of acceptance.

I was in.

November the 26th 1997 I arrived at the training school and wearing my best suit I was ushered into a classroom with twenty nine other nervous souls, ages ranging from 20 to 45. We sat around and made small talk until a sergeant entered and called our names off a clipboard.

"You aren't Police Constables yet, that comes tomorrow, after you are sworn in. Today we'll get your uniforms and do some admin, now let's have a cup of tea and get to know each other."

Most of my shiny new colleagues in the canteen seemed just like me, there were a couple of ex military types who were a bit keener than the rest, but, on the whole, we seemed normal nervous people who were like anyone else on their first day of a new job.

The next day we attended a ceremony at the force H.Q. families in attendance we stood and swore to do our duty, my rough tunic rubbed like a monk's habit and I remember I had a rash on my neck when I got home, the first time I suffered for my job. It wasn't to be the last.

We'd arrived at the address of the reported body and parked in the small car park at the rear.

My notebook says it was 0735hrs and it was just getting light.

I looked up at the low rise flats, they looked like they had been purpose built in the late sixties or early seventies and they had large square windows that looked over a small central garden next to the car park. I looked up and noted a few faces staring back at me, they didn't look away, I did.

A lady in her mid thirties met us as we walked towards the entrance; she was hugging her heavy winter coat around her and wearing slippers at the bottom of bare legs,

"He's by the wall, I've bin shoutin' him, but he hasn't moved." She pointed behind the hedge,

"Do you know who he is love?" I asked, desperate to have an early input and impress my tutor,

"He lives in the ground floor flat, he's a bit of a piss 'ed, he's done it a couple of times now, but he normally wakes up when you shout him."

"Have you shaken him love?" Said Gary, straining to see over the bushes that surrounded the garden,

"I didn't want too; he looks... well he looks strange."

"Okay love, you go in, we'll have a look." said Gary, nodding with his head for me to lead the way.

I found a gap in the bushes and we entered the small garden, it was about forty feet square covered with short neat frost covered grass. Tidy, but empty, flower beds lay at the foot of the bushes, waiting for the weak springtime sun to breathe some life into them. One side butted up tight to the flats, another narrow flower bed, about eighteen inches wide, lay weed free and empty at the foot of the building. Empty, except for a man lying on his back.

Along the wall were ground floor windows to the flats, they were large, old fashioned with cast iron framed picture windows that would have flooded light into living rooms on a summers day. I imagined they'd offer a pleasant view under normal circumstances.

We walked towards him and I called out "Police! Mate, can you hear me?" as per my training. When I bent down next to him he answered that question by looking at me through open, and very dead, eyes.

I'm sitting here now, all these years later and I can still remember those eyes as clear as if I was looking into them right now. We are so used to eyes moving, so used to their flicks and blinks, pupils spreading like oil on water and then slinking back again that we take their life for granted. This was the first time I'd ever seen dead human eyes, and I was still too naive not to know I shouldn't look into them.

You live and learn.

I shone my torch into his face a couple of times and marvelled at the total lack of reaction, my brain struggled for a moment to understand that he couldn't see, those eyes again, tricking me.

"How is he Shoey?"

"He's looks pretty dead to be honest Gary." I said with weak bravado,

"What should we do?"

"Let the control room know?"

"Go on then."

"Delta Romeo 21, control?" My voice quivered a little due to it being so cold, I hoped they didn't think it was because I was nervous. Even though I was scared stiff I didn't want them to know, I was later to learn that hiding nerves is 85% of being a copper, you can do that, you can do anything.

"Delta Romeo 21 go ahead."

"Yeah, we are with this erm... chap in the front garden. It appears that he is erm dead. Over."

"Would you like the Doctor to attend?"

I glanced at Gary who nodded, "Yes please, and erm supervision had best come out as well."

"Roger, can I give a reason for supervision over?"

"Yeah erm..." Gary urged me on with a vigorous nod, "He's in his garden and it maybe needs them to check it out."

"Are you saying it's a suspicious death?"

"No, I'm saying it may be, best safe than sorry thanks."

"Roger... out."

I looked at Gary who smiled and gave me thumbs up.

"Okay, what next?"

"Secure the scene?"

"And where is the scene?"

I looked around at the garden, I could see another gap in the hedge we had missed before, it was closer to the car park entrance and would have been the more direct route to where our deceased unknown male lay.

"That gap in the hedge looks like an entry, maybe there, or maybe the car park?"

"Let's do the car park, the bigger the better."

Gary left to get the tape to seal the scene and I stood over the male. He was wearing a thin dirty lightweight tan coloured overcoat, old nylon trousers and a thin blue shirt. Not much of a barrier to the cold. I felt strange standing there, and almost expected him to move and ask for a hand up. He was, I guessed, maybe in his late seventies. Rough stubble dotted his chin where he hadn't managed to shave properly; it reminded me of marram grass on sand dunes. His lips were parted slightly and I noticed his two front teeth were missing, the rest were yellow and almost matched his coat. Balding, he'd gone down the route of the attempted comb over, and it lay like an abandoned parachute to the left side of his head exposing his pale smooth pate, a final humiliation.

I waited with him for about ten minutes until my Sergeant and the Detective Inspector rolled up. I'd only known Sergeant Scales for a few days; he'd given me the initial impression of a harsh, old-school supervisor. Years later we almost became close and I found him to be a warm, deep thinker, bruised by the job and a failed marriage, but retaining a gentleness and artistic creativity seldom found amongst the ranks of Police supervisors.

"You okay Shoey?" Scales asked, "This your first?"

"I'm sound Sarge." I lied, "It is."

"What's he said?" said the DI.

Big Detective Inspector Ronnie Conroy, it was the first time we'd met and he reminded me of something out of an old seventies crime drama. He was a powerfully built man, long black overcoat blowing open as he walked, immaculately dressed with his grey hair perfectly maintained on his slightly tanned head.

"What's who said?" I replied.

"This fucker." Conroy pointed at my deceased male.

"He's dead Sir, he hasn't said anything."

Conroy bent down and looked at the male, he looked up across the grass and then back at me.

"Come here." Conroy pointed at the spot next to him, I squatted down. "He's dead, but he's still talking, he's telling me he's been here for hours by the frost on his shoes, when you found him were there any footprints other than yours on the grass?"

I looked across at the frost laden grass and remembered that ours had been the first to break through to the green underneath,

"No, ours were the first."

"Look at his hands, only the one closest to the wall has mud on it, which makes me think he fell forward onto the grass, rolled onto his back and into the flowerbed, he's tried to push himself up with his left hand. He's tried a few times because I can see where the soil has moved here." He pointed to a few long furrows pushed in the empty flower bed. "On the wall here, can you see his palm print?" I looked and there it was, a muddy palm print, smeared slightly in a downward motion.

"Have you searched him?"

"No sir."

"Come on then."

I leant over the body.

"No! Lean back, don't get over him, you are dropping all sorts onto him, fibres, skin, you'll end up getting life if we turn him over and he has a fucking big knife sticking out of his back, stay to his sides."

I blushed, and gingerly opened his overcoat and checked his pockets. A dirty hankie, a betting shop pen, tissues and a bottle opener were all I found in the coat. I looked at the DI who nodded for me to continue.

"Do you have rubber gloves Shoey?" Said the Sarge.

"No Sarge."

"Well you will next time won't you."

"Yes Sarge."

I slid my hand into his trousers pocket, I could feel the cold flesh through the material and it reminded me of a job I'd once had that involved unloading meat wagons. It surprised me that a dead human and a dead cow felt the same, it shouldn't have surprised me... but it did.

In his trousers I found his wallet, I emptied it onto the grass next to me. In the Police we called them "personal papers", in real life I saw a photo of a little girl, maybe two inches square, black and white with a thick cream coloured crease breaking through the middle, splitting her in half. I wondered if she was about to tore in half again.

There was a bus pass, it told me the name of the deceased, and he stared at me with the same eyes out from his bus pass. Photo booth vanity had ensured his hair was in place and his top shirt button was fastened, I did some maths, he was only sixty two, no age to be lying dead in a garden.

"That's the lot Sir, personal papers and about six quid in change."

"Any keys?"

"No."

Conroy stood up and studied the male and then looked at the building.

"Is that the only door in?"

"Yep." said the Sarge.

Conroy walked along the flowerbed and pulled at the adjacent closed windows one by one, until finally, about fifteen feet from us, one swung open. He stuck his head inside and shouted,

"Hello!". Nobody replied.

"This will be his, come here."

I joined him and looked into the flat, it was sparsely furnished, two armchairs and a dirty couch. The couch cushions looked like wafers and at its base was an assortment of cheap cider and beer cans. Newspaper littered the floor and the smell was a mix of dirty socks and alcohol.

"In you go." Nodded the DI and I did as I was told.

I called out as I wandered through the flat; I quickly established that the living room was the most luxurious. In the kitchen I found several bottles of tablets and uncollected prescriptions, our deceased hadn't been a well man; I scooped up the prescriptions and made a note of the tablets.

In the hallway by a dirty yellow landline telephone I found a personal phone book, one of those pre mobile phone ones with letters cut away down the side. I flipped through it and noted how the handwriting had changed over the years; a careful copperplate hand had been replaced by a lazy scrawl, often the names didn't correspond with the pages given letter, I guessed they had made sense to someone, once. Next to the phone lay some house keys.

I rejoined the DI at the window,

"I've got a number for his Doctor, and a few that might be family, his kitchen is full of tablets as well Sir, he wasn't a well man."

"Well if he was, he certainly isn't now, good work Shoey, out you come, the Doctor is here."

I climbed out and saw Gary and the Doctor examining the body, I was glad I'd been in the kitchen when he arrived else it would have been my bare hands rolling him over and lifting up his shirt.

"The neighbour has told me he was an alcoholic who was always forgetting his keys, he used to leave the window open and step back into the flat when he got home, if he was too drunk to manage stepping in he'd just sleep in the garden until he sobered up." Said the Sarge

"It's easy enough to get in; the sill is only about eighteen inches high." I replied.

"It was a miracle he could manage that, looks like he had cirrhosis, there is a lot of fluid retention, he has ulcers on his legs. I'd guess he was experiencing acute liver failure." The Doctor said without looking up.

"Not very cute from here." said Gary, he was holding the male on his side and there was the foul smell of failed bowels.

"He will have done that just before he died." Said the Doctor.

"I wish he would have waited." replied Gary and we all smiled, despite ourselves, I was already getting that black sense of humour that follows the emergency services around.

I showed the Doctor the list of medication I'd found, he nodded and stood up.

"Heart problems, liver problems and a few more things to boot, this looks like he has been drinking, walked home, fallen, possibly due to drink, possibly to his other ailments. He's been compos mentis to know it's too cold to stay outside and he has struggled to get up. I'd suggest at this stage he's had heart failure, maybe before he fell, or during his struggle to get up and that has caused his death.

Either way, I'm happy to say in my opinion there have been no suspicious circumstances."

DI Conroy nodded and brushed down the front of his immaculate overcoat, content that it was "case closed".

"Shut the scene lads, get the undertakers out and get him shifted see if you can find out his next of kin Shoey, save the coroners lads a job."

Minutes later I found myself again alone with my first pudding. Everyone else had packed away, the Sarge and the DI back on their way to the nick, Gary collecting the crime scene tape and the Doctor writing up his notes in the warmth of his Volvo.

I remained with the sad old man, his shirt still open, milky white hairless chest exposed to the cold morning air. It was getting fully light and many of the neighbours had drawn their curtains to shield them from the scene.

"Do you want a cup of tea love?"

I jumped, an elderly ladies head was popping out of an upstairs window, rollers in she looked down upon us like a geriatric Juliet.

"No thanks love, we'll not be here much longer." I replied, covering my nervous jump of moments before.

"It's very sad," she replied, "he used to be a lovely man, the drink got hold of him, it's such a shame."

I nodded as she closed the window and went back to her warm kitchen, and then I knelt and did up his shirt and pulled his coat across his chest.

Such a shame.

30. Ignoring The Fuel Light.

"You mate is on the telly." Said Terry as he walked towards me carrying my sixth lager of an impressively early night.

"Who?" I craned my neck to look up and around the pillar which I was leaning against for moral support.

I expected to see an episode of Crimewatch, but it wasn't, it was John Bishop on a chat show, looking all toothy and trendy as he made people laugh with his constant looks of amazement and despair.

I sighed and took my pint from Terry and turned away from the TV.

"He's not my mate."

"You said he was!"

"I didn't. I said I'd gigged with him once, years ago, and that he was an alright bloke."

"You were in that shite film with him!"

"I was in a film he was in... we never appeared together, unless you count the bit where they had sandbags in the coffin he was supposed to be in. They didn't use the stuff when we were together... because it was shite."

"You said he was your mate."

"I didn't." I said to my pint.

"Just think... that could be you." Terry said to me.

He gazed up at the screen behind me and supped his drink before nodding his head for me to take a look. I sighed, looked, sighed again, and looked away.

Bishop was chatting with some gorgeous Hollywood starlet and making her chuckle with his scouse charm while I was talking to a moron in a pub.

"I was as good as him." I mumbled to my pint as I put it to my lips, unfortunately Terry, and not my pint, answered.

"Of course you were."

"I was!" With conviction. "On my day." I added, with slightly less conviction.

"Are you telling me you were as funny as John Bishop when you did comedy?"

"Well... well I had my moments..." Even less conviction this time.

"Are you telling me you were as funny as John Bishop when you did comedy?" he asked again, this time with a look that said "bollocks" without actually saying it.

"Erm... well maybe not as consistently funny but..."

"So why isn't that you up there then?"

I looked up at the screen then back at my Friday night pint,

"I don't know, maybe he wanted it more?"

Later as I walked home I thought why Bishop was living the dream while I walked home to a dingy house with a dog who would be desperate for a wee (hopefully, or I was scrubbing the carpet again) I wondered why he was on the telly, and I was struggling to pay the telly licence.

Is it just talent? Is it hard work plus talent? Is it luck? I can remember some comics who could reduce a room to tears with tales of their life, I'd seen them do it once or twice then never seen them again. I'd ask promoters what had happened to them and they would shrug and say things like,

"Dunno, think they packed in." Or "they got a bird/bloke." Just before saying "We did agree fifteen quid and you are on second after that student who has brought all his mates."

Maybe it's drive, the ability to just keep going when your fuel light blinks on, to keep pushing when others give up.

Which is why me and comedy broke up and I swore never to see her again, I left her to carry on seeing John Bishop and Alan Carr behind my back while I pretended we'd never gone out in the first place. But the problem with Comedy is that she is a cruel mistress, because after you've gone out together for a while, made love a few times and then broke up, she keeps sending you texts asking "Can you do a cheeky ten?"

And like all losers in love and life, I say,

"Yes."

That's why I found myself waiting to go on at a gig run in a pub last week, for the first time in eighteen months.

Did they laugh?

Yes.

Did I enjoy it?

Yes.

Am I the new John Bishop?

If I put my mind to it... well... truth be told, probably not.

But it's more fun doing a gig than watching him do one, if only for me and not my audience.

31. A Liverpool Tapestry.

Liverpool, shiny and bright, a city centre that twinkles and winks with lights like a pretty girl in a nightclub who's just smiled at you across the dance floor. On a Saturday night it throbs with life, it's a wasp's nest, where the wasps wear six inch heels and have vodka in their handbags and teeter and totter all false nails and false tan.

Skirts are short, nightclub queues are long and instead of last orders they have the last post when the final drinkers fall in battle on a Sunday morning, mown down by drunk tanks instead of enemy tanks.

"Love Liverpool, love life" the slogan once said, I'd agree, although I'd probably swap "lager" for "life" on a Saturday night.

Let me explain, I used to drive a private hire taxi in Liverpool, what some of you would call a mini cab. What started out as a job, done to get me through some hard times when I was at rock bottom, became something very different. Driving a cab changed me, it opened my eyes and lifted my senses, it taught me about people, and, more importantly, about myself.

You see, all around us are little dramas; they might not resonate like Darfur, or Damascus. They'll never scratch the surface of the news, they are important only to the people they affect, each one a tiny Everest to be climbed and overcome. What might seem trivial to you might be a monster under the bed to me. Pushing and prodding and keeping me awake all night, tossing and turning the troubles in my mind until the birds sing outside... the cheerful bastards.

When I used to look out the window at Liverpool on a Saturday night, reflected light from neon nightclubs bouncing off the glass like the boom boom of the beat outside, I didn't see teetering beauties and badgering boys. I used to see a million and one stories in the half naked city, waiting to be written by me.

We all like to think we are special.

Deep down, in that little place where we talk to ourselves and nobody else can hear, we like to think we make a difference, that things wouldn't be the same if we weren't here. Most of us would never say it out loud of course, we'll never admit it, but come on, it's true. We all like to think that when we die someone will put up a statue to celebrate and remember us, and that dad's will crouch down with little boys and point and tell tales about us, keeping our flame alive when we have burnt out.

We all like to think like that, don't we?

The sad fact is that we'll pass this way with barely a whisper, forgotten after one breath of a milleniums grief.

Maybe a memory on a photograph, somebody pointing at a dusty album.

We are fallen leaves on the banks of the Amazon, beautiful while we lasted, but soon floating away, unnoticed, let alone remembered, washed out to sea... gone.

Our drama forgotten, washed away in the swirl of world news and space probes, our teeny tiny torment never heard, unimportant to everyone except us, and yet without these torments, without these personal tales, the tapestry of 21st century Britain will never be complete. Behind the headlines we are all in the background, doing our bit, making the kingdom united.

These are three of those tiny stories, three hours, three dramas, three threads in one Saturday night, modern Britain, modern Liverpool far away from the shiny city centre, hold them to your ear like a sea shell, and listen as they capture the sound in the pool of life.

....

I was sitting drinking cold coffee listening to cars smash through puddles making noises like a cymbals crashing. The night was sticky hot and humid, unlike my coffee, and my arm was out the window when my cars computer called to tell me someone had somewhere to go.

I pulled up at the fast food restaurant with a heavy heart; fast food on a late night usually meant a drunken dribbling oaf who had ordered too many munchies after too many beers. I was relieved to see a fifty something bloke in the company uniform come out, he had a doggy bag of supper and as he climbed into the car and I got a whiff of cooking fat and grease that would have every dog in Liverpool drooling.

He pushed back his baseball cap and told me where he was going then offered me a burger out of his bag,

"No thanks mate, trying to stay off them, got to watch your weight in this job."

"I can't stand them but I'm starving, I had to eat something it's been a long day."

I smiled; the salesman was off duty as he peered into the brown paper bag and scrunched up his nose,

"Do you mind if I eat one?" He asked, and I shook my head in a "fire away" sort of way.

The bag rustled and out came a cheeseburger, it looked worse in the mirror than it smelt in my nose and he unwrapped, stared at it, then shook his head and put it back.

His was not a happy meal.

"I'm sick of looking at them, fourteen hours today I've been flogging these bleedin' things."

"Fourteen hours?"

"Yeah, I did some overtime, I could have stayed on all night but I've got an interview tomorrow so I wanted to get home."

"An interview? Don't you fancy sticking out them fourteen hour days?" I teased him because I already knew the answer; he shook his head and smiled a reply.

"I'm desperate to get out, only been there two months. I'm an engineer by trade, I ended up there because the dole sent me. I couldn't get anything else."

"An engineer? Flipping burgers?"

"I got finished up last year, not worked for nearly twelve months and they were going to stop my money, I had to do something."

"Bloody hell, leaving aside the job, that must have been a hell of a drop in money?"

"That's why I'm working so late, only way to make ends meet, we can't sell the house so we work every hour to pay for it, my missus is working in a supermarket nights as well."

"Don't you get help with your mortgage? I thought the government had a fund set up for people like you?"

"We don't get anything, all those years working for nice things and bang... you get finished up and the lot is nearly lost in the space of six months. I don't know how much longer we'll be able to hold on."

"Maybe you'd better off letting go and starting again?"

"No, I've worked hard for what I've got, I'm going to fight for it, I just need to get this job tomorrow..." He trailed off and I let him go, we drove on listening to a football phone in on the radio, people talking about millionaires who "don't try hard enough".

I pulled up at a nice house in a nice street and my engineer paid me in silver and copper from weighed down pockets on a weighed down man.

He opened the door and said,

"You sure you don't want a burger?"

"No honestly, I'm fine thanks, good luck tomorrow."

"Cheers, I'll need it."

He screwed up the bag, looked like neither of us were eating them, they were bin bound, a bit like he'd be if he didn't get that job in the morning.

....

"Onward and upward" was something my dad used to like saying, he would throw it into conversation on a regular basis, encouraging me to strive, reach for the stars, keep climbing.

My next two passengers were definitely "upward", they were so "upward" they barely knew what day it was.

They were higher than kites.

"Cheers lad, we're going to..." The first one trailed off as I silently thanked god my window was open. The smell of skunk cannabis flooded the car to the extent I thought my Magic tree was going to storm off in a huff.

"Yeah?" I waited for direction from the directionless.

"We're going to..." Time ticked, like a bomb, and I was about to explode.

"Hmm?" I looked in the mirror at his blank face; next to him his mate stared at a cheap mobile phone screen and ignored the two of us.

"Going to..."

"Come on mate, I haven't got all night." My temper frayed, tiredness was pulling at my loose threads and I was starting to unravel.

"Where are we going?" Stoner one looked at Stoner two who looked up from his phone and looked at Stoner one like they'd just met, before looking at me, and then back at his mate.

"Kayleigh's you dick 'ed."

Stoner one looked at me and I inwardly swore to myself that if he said "Kayleigh's" to me I was going to climb over the seat and beat the pair of them to death with my A to Z.

His mouth moved like a goldfish for a second then eventually he summoned up an address from his fog filled brain that was slumped in the corner of his skull like a hippy in a squat party.

I shook my head and pulled away.

"Had a good night lad?" Stoner one enquired in a drawl that made John Wayne sound like Rex Harrison.

"Quiet lad." I replied; never keen to let my takings be exposed to the perusal of two scallies after midnight. "What about you two? Been watching University Challenge?"

Stoner one smiled in the mirror at my cheeky joke and shook his head,

"Nah lad, playin' the playstation and that, chillin' 'avin' a smoke."

"I can smell the weed, have you saved some or is that coming out your pores?"

Both Stoners laughed the laugh of the stoned and Stoner one fished in his pocket and produced some buds of skunk in a plastic envelope.

"Eee ear lad, do you want some?" He offered me the envelope and I shook my head, thinking that these two would have enjoyed the now bin bagged burgers from earlier.

"No thanks mate, I'm too old for the sort of thing."

"Behave mate! You are never too old for a smoke! This is good weed this, we grow it ourselves..." He opened the envelope so as to offer me the proof of his labours and the car filled with the foul stench of the mighty herb that conquered all.

"Oh mate shut the fucking envelope please! If the bizzies drive past they'll pull me over!" I pleaded and the stoner complied, shuffling the packet back into his black nylon tracksuit pocket with a smile and a shrug, no offence taken or intended he opened his window an inch to let the fumes out.

We drove on a while, after stopping at a late night off licence to buy some cider that came in a bottle the size of a diver's oxygen tank and was the colour of urine. The we carried on driving, listening to some late night DJ prattle on. I'd changed the station to suit my passengers, modern music for the modern mind, both brain numbed in their own way.

Stoner one spoke to Stoner two,

"She'd better be in lad, or I'm gonna smash her tomorrow."

I glanced at my clock; it was nearly two am,

"She might be in bed?" I offered, happy to turn back and to make more money.

"No lad, she rung sayin' she couldn't sleep, she's took some "garys" and needs a smoke to calm her down."

"Mission of mercy then?" I replied and he smiled back.

In Liverpool a "gary" is a tablet, (named after the ex Liverpool and Everton, recently deceased, footballer, Gary Ablett, (Ablett=tablet? Geddit?). Young people buy them for a few quid not knowing what they are getting, someone will turn up, take their money and push two or three (if you are lucky) "garys" into your sweaty palm. You don't know what they are and you certainly don't know what they will do, you just take them, and hope they will "work".

Sunday mornings were the dreaded "gary" hours for me, people whizzing and fizzing after taking nine or ten of the things in the course of a few hours, talking at a million miles an hour, mood swinging ear ringing top of the voice singing walking nightmares I couldn't wait to kick out.

Give me weed smashed stoners any day of the week.

We pulled up in the tiny terraced street of two up two downs, Kayleigh sat on the doorstep sucking on a cigarette. Her front door was open and I could see straight into her living room, on the TV was a music channel where a rapper was surrounded by semi naked dance girls on a beach somewhere.

It was a million miles from the puddles and peddlers of a dark damp Liverpool night.

She stood up in her pyjamas and Ugg boots and shuffled towards the car as Stoner one fished in his pocket and passed me a scrunched up twenty pound note for a five pound fare,

"Take a tenner lad." He lolled as he spoke, trying to be the rapper he wasn't and looking to impress Kayleigh, who was standing by his window, pushing lank blonde hair out of panda eyes with stubby fingers topped with chewed nails splashed with cheap polish.

"I'm going to fuckin' smash her." Stoner two spoke, the most animated he'd been the entire journey.

I passed over the tenner and stoner one thanked me, before he got out he tapped me on the shoulder,

"You sure you don't want a smoke? On the house?"

"No thanks." I replied, even though I felt like I could do with one.

....

It was hammering down and dark. Rain that sounded like a thousand suicidal frogs was landing on the roof of my car and although I was inside, I felt damp. Damp from all the passengers I'd had that night, steaming and humid after summer showers that came thick and fast and charged down dry gutters like paint down the side of a tin.

I stared at the front door of the shabby semi that hid behind a privet hedge, the sort of hedge nobody plants anymore. The kind that someone with braces used to cut in the fifties, it had once been square, shoulders straight, but now it slouched, like a green Chelsea Pensioner when the Queen drives past, doing its best to remind us what once was.

I looked at my clock, it was coming up to three, time marched on and I was still only halfway to my bed.

I looked at the house again, and it stared back, blankly a million miles from the bouncing a booming shiny city centre of new Liverpool, I was in the suburbs, a different place where we are told thirty percent of houses are full of people not working, I knew those houses. I'd lived in one once upon a time.

Being a private hire taxi driver involves a lot of looking at houses, I've sat staring at more tungsten lit terraces than I care to remember. It got that way I could tell by the curtains who was going to come out, I could tell you if a pensioner would wobble down the path or a coke fuelled young exec, just by the amount of light coming off the telly or the shape of a vase on the window sill.

As much as I read the Liverpool Echo when it was quiet, I read the Liverpool houses when it was busy.

I wasn't surprised to see the middle aged black lady in a blue carer's uniform come out the paint peeled front door and dodge the rain drops as she ran down the path.

It is a sad fact now that so many of our elderly sit in darkened rooms waiting to be put to bed by strangers every night. Given tablets and wet flannelled faces by someone you've never met before, who only knows your name because it's written on a file by the door is a grim reality for people who deserve so much better.

The carers work for pennies, long hours and long faces, wiping chins and places unmentioned. I've spoke to girls who had barely left school who would help old lonely men into pyjamas after baths, rushing to get to the next one, no time to talk, no time to listen, tablets and toast and then the next one ticked off.

No time to think, thank god.

My black lady fell into the car and let out a laugh,

"Argggh! I'm so wet!" She shouted and I smiled in my mirror and waited for her to settle, she shuffled around and flicked at her hair, "I forgot my umbrella this morning and I have been rained on so many times."

"This morning? Have you been working all day?" I glanced at the clock again, suddenly not feeling so sorry for myself.

"I left me home at eleven thirty; it has been a loooong day."

She spoke in the West African way that always made me feel lazy about my scouse, picking out her words and making them sound complete, little tongue chiselled pieces of perfection.

"So where are we going now? Home?"

"No, I have one more lady to see, I am running very late, one of the other carers has quit tonight and they do not have any cover except me."

I shook my head and she gave me the address, it was about three miles away so I started to splash my way there wipers a blur, same as the night outside.

"So you've been working over twelve hours?"

"Thirteen and a half, I am very tired, but my manager had nobody else to do the work."

"There must be someone else, it isn't fair to ask you to do all this, you must be exhausted?"

"I am back to work again tomorrow at nine in the morning, it needs to be done, besides, I am glad of the extra money, caring doesn't pay me much, and when it gets to this time of the night I have to pay for you too."

"Doesn't the company pay for the taxis?"

"They will only pay for buses."

"But there aren't any buses at this time of the night!"

She smiled and shrugged in the mirror and I watched her face flush different colours in the glare of a midnight traffic light, red, amber, green.

"What time do you normally finish?"

"It depends on buses, and whether other people are running late, but I normally work twelve hours, getting home at midnight, my little girl never sees me when I am working. It is very hard on my husband also; he has to get up very early for his own job."

"What does he do?"

"He is working in a factory, putting things in boxes; he works very long hours also. He is an educated man and he gets very depressed, it's very hard on all of us."

"I know how he feels, being depressed that is, makes you wonder what the point of it all is?" I replied shaking my head at the grimness of it all.

"We do it for our daughter, so her life will be better; she has a future here, better than when we lived in Nigeria... we do it for her."

She smiled and shrugged then looked out the window, I looked at her reflection as she reflected, and I wondered what light there was at the end of the tunnel for her. What was she working towards? It is sad when your only hope is the hope of a better life for your daughter who hardly knows you, when you don't expect your own future to improve, what chance has your child got.

It's difficult to enjoy your child's smile when your eyes are closed with exhaustion.

Modern Britain, waiting for it to get better, taking the pain so our children will gain but losing ourselves in the process.

We all like to think we can make a difference, maybe together we can?

32. Purdy's Gig.

Many years ago, when I was full of vim and vigour, I was rung up by a mate called Dave Purdy to play his gig in Manchester. Now I had heard about this place, many comics spoke of it in hushed tones as being a bit of a hell hole.

Only a few weeks before a punter had been thrown out of the pub for threatening to beat up one of the acts, he'd then thrown a bottle through the window after his ejection and had caused a massive fight in the car park. So all in all it's fair to say I wasn't much looking forward to the gig and should really have made some excuse and not gone. But Dave was a bit of a comedy guru, not just to me, but to just about every comic who came out of Manchester around that time, at some point in your early open spot phase you would end up sat opposite Dave with a bottle of red between you as he smoked a rolled up cigarette. Occasionally he would jab his tab at you like some sort of drunken smoking wasp as he ripped you to bits, that rolly and the words that huskily followed it were worse than any wasp.

I remember him pouring some wine into my empty pint glass as he offered me the following piece of advice,

"You were shit, but you didn't have to be, don't be such a lazy fucker and get your finger out."

Now those of you who know me will know that I'm not the kind of person who takes kindly to be called "shit", but, as usual, Dave was right, and it's hard to take umbridge with someone who you know is right. So I drunk my lagerwine (he hadn't noticed I still had half an inch of Carling in the bottom of my glass) and nodded and took it on the chin from someone who knew comedy.

So the day Dave rung me to ask would I do his gig I have to be honest I really wanted to say no.

So I did.

"You... are a lazy fuuuucker Shoey, I knew you were, I fuuuucking told you the other day."

"I know Dave, but to be honest it sounds like a terrible gig and I can't be bothered driving for an hour to do a terrible gig."

"You aren't driving to do a terrible gig, you are driving to do a brilliant gig."

"But everyone has told me it's terrible."

"Yeah, but you'll make it brilliant if you want too."

On that note I ummed and aaaahed for a bit and

then said

"Alright, but if it's crap I'm not doing it again, and I don't want to hear you moan about it, okay?"

"It won't be crap... it'll be brilliant."

On that note, later that night, I found myself driving around deepest darkest Manchester searching for the pub the gig was held in (This was pre sat-nav times in the days when reading an A-Z resting in your lap on the motorway was part of your driving test).

I finally turned up at a pub that looked like Hitler's bunker in Downfall. A truly bleak mix of concrete and graffiti that even its mother couldn't love.

I opened the door and wandered past more nylon tracksuits than were at the Montreal Olympics and found Dave and some other comics at the end of the bar. Dave was pissed but in good spirits and quickly introduced me to some of the comics and the pub manager. He went onto tell me that seeing as I had come furthest he would put me on first. He pointed to the stage (which was a few beer crates and some hardboard) and said,

"They will love you here Shoey, they like people who are like them."

I tried not to take offence as I glanced around the bar,

"Don't worry I'll give you a big build up, come on let's get going."

The other comics nodded support as Dave made his way to the mic. I watched as my colleagues swallowed nervously, their Adams apples bobbing like it was Halloween, each one of them glad they weren't me.

I told myself that I should just get on and get it over with, "how bad could it be?"

Dave did a few minutes and then gave me tiny nod of the head as warning I was about to go on,

"Our first act is a great comic, he's new to the circuit but I'm certain you are going to like him... He's from Liverpool..."

Cue massive jeers and my Adams apple joining in with everyone else's in a synchronised bobbing session,

"No! come on! He's a cracking lad, as I said, he's a scouser and he is also a copper (more jeers, more bobbing)... so let's have a warm welcome for Tony Schumacher!"

To say that I got a warm welcome was an understatement. You'd get a cooler welcome at the gates of Hell when the air conditioning was playing up. I can remember glancing across to the bar at one point and seeing the barmaid watching, she had her hand to her mouth and looked like someone who was watching a puppy get run over.

All in all it was a bit like an out of body experience, like one of those people who calmly watch Doctors pound on their chest from the corner of the ceiling.

Except I wasn't calm, I was shitting myself.

Poor Dave died a few years back, that night I think I knew how he felt.

Why, you ask (assuming you are asking) are you telling me this?

Well, the other week I turned up at a gig and had a similar feeling. Except this one was in Liverpool and I am no longer a copper (although I am still a lazy fkr).

The gig had been organised by a comedy mate, who keeps encouraging me out of the cab and back onto the stage. It was being held at the Bleak House Pub in Dingle, Liverpool. For those of you who don't know it,

Dingle is a rough, old fashioned, working class neighbourhood in Liverpool.

Most of the people who live there come from families who have lived in the area for generations. They have had it tough and are tough. It would be fair to say that Capital Of Culture didn't venture out this far from the city centre because it would have been too scared it would be mugged if it had.

The Bleak House pub looks just like it's name suggests, local folk claim that Charles Dickens lived in the area when he moved to Liverpool with the intention of sampling the underbelly of the city. I don't know if he did or not, but if it was underbelly Chas was after, underbelly was what he would have found. This place had more underbelly than Michelle McManus.

The landlord looked (and probably was) a real hard case, but he was welcoming and enthusiastic, as was John, the guy who had organised the gig.

"Shoey you will rip it here, they will love you because you're like them." He said.

"Where have I heard that before?" I thought "Purdy will be pissing himself if he can see this."

"I'm putting you on first mate, you'll get them going."

"Only thing going will be me," I thought, "to the toilet."

The time to go on came, the compère had done a stellar job battling against the noise and boisterous crowd, I say boisterous, it was like a Munich Beer Hall just after they found out Mike And Bernie Winters were the cabaret.

Up I went, heckles abounded, noisy talkers gabbed, tills slammed and glasses chinked and I worked my arse off. After a couple of minutes I got into that place only comics know, the place where you feel like you are surfing a wave and every word is met with a nod and a laugh.
I danced around heckles like Errol Flynn did with Basil Rathbone, darting and parrying and swinging from chandeliers of dazzling wit.

My time drew to a close and I pulled my act around me like Matador would his cape, my closing line delivered like a sword to an exhausted bull's spine... deadly, precise, final.

When I stepped from the stage I felt as if on air, hand clapped and shoulder patted I rested against the bar to watch the rest of the show.

A lady at the bar turned to me, smiled and

beckoned me closer, I leant in close and smelled her perfume, "I've worked the old magic," I thought "Women love men who can make them laugh."

She drew her mouth close to my ear, I felt her hairspray stiffened hair brush my cheek and smelt the Blue WKD on her breath, she gasped, husky with foreign cigarettes and red nails resting on my forearm like five randy mosquitoes, and whispered softly,

"You should tell more jokes."

The cow.

33. Forever In Your debt.

I'm not in the habit of quoting Shakespeare to people, I've always had a sneaking suspicion that people who quote Shakespeare are the kind of people who buy books for their coffee table and only open them when they hear the doorbell. You know the sort, the ones who used to fold the News of the World up inside The Observer.

But I'm going to break my rule just this once, safe in the knowledge that I don't have a coffee table and the NOTW has gone the way of a deleted voicemail message, so here goes:

"Wouldst thou have a serpent sting thee twice?"

This popped into my head a few months back, it was long lazy afternoon of staring out of my private hire taxi windscreen and waiting for a fare. I was close to home and I could hear the couch and the kettle calling me but I'd told myself whatever happened I was going to sit tight for ten hours, even if that did mean prolonged periods of resting my head on the steering wheel as my day went down like a slow puncture.

When I finally got a job I felt like Daniel Day Lewis when he struck oil in There Will Be Blood, I fired up the focus and bolted around to the rough old neighbourhood where my salvation lay. The second the door opened I knew my new found hope had been misplaced.

Mum and Daughter supported each other down the path like conjoined twins on ice. Mum must have been seventy plus, she looked like a skeleton wrapped in wet parchment. Her neck barely thick enough to hold up her head and you could have used her fingers to pick a lock they were so thin. Her hair was like rusted wire wool glue to the end of a pencil and the clumpy flat black shoes wouldn't have looked out of place on Frankenstein's monster.

The daughter was maybe my age, a fragile soul set in a fast food frame. Bulky and track suited her pasty face had the colour of fresh dough, and, I'm afraid to say, the consistency. Daughter's eyes darted this way and that, the caution of someone who thinks the outdoors isn't so great.

I knew they weren't going far before they even got in, in every sense of the phrase.

Daughter bundled herself into the back seat and slid across with all the grace of a skittish hippo, her mum got in after her and helped her daughter settle. I realised this was a woman who had not only given birth, but given her life, to her child. I could feel the weight of her burden as she clucked, cooed and calmed her daughter who in turn fought with her seatbelt and talked at a gallop.

"How does this work, I can never work these things, I pull and pull. Are you okay mate? Sorry mate. How does this work? Mum? Pull that?" She rattled away like a machine gun all twists and yanks and fingers to her face, it was like watching a pan of water about to boil over.

My heart ached as Mum settled her in and then turned to me and, over a sound track of chatter from her daughter asked to go to Huyton Village.

I sighed, less than a mile, £2.20, that job working in McDonalds looked more and more appealing as I pulled away from the kerb then felt guilty as Mum apologised,

"I'm sorry it's only a short one, we can't walk far."

"It's alright love, you tell me where to go and I go there, that's my job."

I smiled in the mirror and she smiled back, the lines on her face momentarily giving me a clue to what she had once looked like.

"We're going to sort out her money, aren't we?"

"Yeah, yeah, bloody robbers, robbers they are, yeah. I only lent £150, bloody robbers, robbers aren't they mum?"

"She only lent £150, they've been phoning me for weeks about it, she's been in hospital, hasn't been able to pay have you love?"

"No, no, I've been in hospital, not been well. I was in hospital."

I glanced in the mirror and Mum rolled her eyes and I nodded a reply, getting the message. Her daughter still wasn't well, she was twisting and turning in a mental storm and she was a long way from the shore, battered by breakers and break downs she was clinging to her mother for dear life. I've seen those break downs close up before, messy affairs that leave no stone unturned, nightmares come to life as the world towers around, looming and pushing you down into the pit and I only hoped her mother had the strength to pull her out.

"So who has been phoning you?"

"This bloody loan company, they never leave me alone." Said Mum, "She had to give them my number when she took the loan out."

"Have you guaranteed the money?"

"No, they just phone and phone asking where she is, chasing her until she pays them."

"I've already given them three hundred haven't I mum?"

"She has, she still owes them one hundred."

"For £150? Bloody hell that's robbery!"

"I'm taking out a loan to pay it off, to reduce the payments." Said Mum, stuck between a rock and a hard up place.

The shopping centre the women were going to was one of those ones built in the 70's to look modern, they would have called it a "New development" but if anything it was a step backwards. Like something from a North Korean planning manual it was all grey concrete, mildew and to-let signs with sausage roll wrappers blowing around like tumble weed.

I know "the village" well, I grew up around there, it was once an exciting place for young Schumacher, my Mum would take my dads pay-packet and we'd wander around paying bills on a Saturday morning, first to the Gas Board, then to the Water Board, then maybe the telly rental and then to the shops. The envelope getting thinner but the money there to see, to be held and spent till it was gone. We didn't have credit cards, if we didn't have money we didn't have money. I got a comic on a Saturday and thirty minutes in the library to look for an Agaton Sax book or maybe something by Bill Naughton. They weren't coffee table books; they were under bed sheet books, lit by a torch not a Habitat lamp.

There must be four or five "Cheque Shops" and "Payday Loan" outlets dotted around the charity shops and shutters in the Village now. The council charge for parking so there is a Russian Steppe of a space were cars once waited, like the great plains after the buffalo had gone. All those cars are parked at the nearby mega store which enjoys a huge free car park that was donated by the same council that now is choking off the independent retailer.

I watched the two women wobble off to indenture themselves and their benefits to the serpent that would no doubt be stinging them more than twice. I wondered where it had all gone wrong since Blair and Brown told us "Things can only get better" and Obama wittered and twittered on about "change".

It funny how as we watch Europe nobody really seems to mention the little people struggling with debts of their own.

It appears the only interest is the kind that charges 1000%.

34. John Lennon is dead.

I'm not a morning person, never have been either. I'm more likely to be accused of being a bit of a nark, than being up with the lark. So the morning that my Mum burst into my bedroom, threw open the curtains and said,

"John Lennon's dead."

Two things struck me,

"Why are you opening the curtains? It's still dark outside." Closely followed by,

"Who cares if John Lennon is dead?"

I went downstairs and had cornflakes with freezing cold milk; this was in the days when your front step was colder than your fridge, the rest of the family were glued to Radio City who were breaking the news. But I sat munching, disinterested, safe in the knowledge that The Beatles were old fashioned and Lennon was rubbish.

I pretty much got myself ready for school and off I set to walk to my mate Terry's house. When I arrived he solemnly beckoned me in and ushered me into the kitchen. As I sat waiting for him (I may have even pinched a biscuit) I flicked through the night before's Liverpool Echo and listened to the usual early morning household hubbub. After a while and during a lull I heard the sound of sobbing. Proper full on deep can't get your breath sorrowful sobs of sadness.

After a few minutes Terry joined me pulling his tie over his head,

"Who's crying?"

"Our Karen."

"Why?"

"John Lennon's dead."

It took me years to understand why she was crying, and then one night, having had a few beers, I sat in my families' front room with head phones on while everyone else slept. Boxes of old albums had been emptied and picked through, everything from Jim Reeves to Deaf School. Eventually I stumbled across Lennon's "Julia", scratchy and sad, a love song for someone lost.

And I knew how Karen felt.

35. The Futurist Cinema.

The futurist used to flutter her eyelashes at me as I sat in traffic on Lime Street for years. You see, back then I was a taxi driver, one of the exalted few allowed to drive from south to north on Lime Street who wouldn't get a ticket from the tall skinny cameras that sat opposite the Adelphi.

I'd often sit waiting for the lights to change looking at the crumbling dangerous facades opposite, not the buildings that is, I'm talking about the smokers standing outside the Yankee bar. But occasionally, the traffic would be backed up so far that I'd have to wait opposite The Futurist. I'd rest my chin in my hand, sigh, and stare up at what looked like a haunted house, shuttered and shattered. Suicidal bushes clinging onto the gutters with a few scruffy pigeons staring back at me, looking for a fight, or a flight, it was hard too tell.

It was one such winters rush hour that I saw her winking at me, lazily fluttering silver strand eyelashes looking for love, drowning in despair and trying to catch the eye of a passerby, a passerby like me.

"Look at that." I said to my half drunk passenger in the back.

"What?"

"Up there on the left, first floor, those silver strands are blowing out of the broken window. They must have been fancy curtains or something, they look like eyelashes..."

He didn't reply, I thought he was lost in the romance of the moment just like me,

"Do you know what time the lap dancing club shuts?" He said from the back.

I suppose we aren't all romantics after all.

I can only remember one film I saw in The Futurist, it was called Hanger 18 and it was rubbish, I mean really rubbish. Me and my mate Terry went to see it, I reckon I was about fourteen, nobody checked my age when I bought a ticket, nobody cared, same as nobody really cared when the place closed shortly after.

I got a job a few years later working in a jewellers on Mount Pleasant, that was almost as crap as the film, although slightly less predictable. I used to pass the Futurist as I headed home every night, the pair of us shuttered up and not noticed, miserable, wet with rain and stoic, assigned to our roles, her as a symbol of a cities decay and me a reminder that not trying at school led to dull jobs.

She didn't wink at me then, she still had her dignity, and glass in her windows. She looked like a middle aged Miss Haversham, waiting for her long lost lover to come back and throw up her shutter and fire up her projectors. He didn't come; he was too busy having a night in playing with his video recorder.

The eighties passed, Heseltine and Hatton and came and went, the nineties rolled into to town and her makeup slid down her face a few inches more. Somewhere along the line her windows broke and some letters dropped off her name like memories from a dementia sufferer. They left ghostly grime outlines, shadows of the past, almost forgotten like the building they'd once hung on.

The pigeons and seagulls moved in, not Walter and George, they'd long gone, these were the type that crapped everywhere and let feathers fall from the ceiling, slower than the chunks of plaster they dislodged.

I moved on, did different things, she just stood there, waiting at the bus stop, next to arcades, then the night clubs and then the half naked women. The smell of kebabs wafting past her nose, she squinted, eye sight failing, memory faded, fluttering her eyelash on her one good eye she waited at the bus stop for people to get off and warm her up.

But they didn't.

One day I got a phone call off a flickeringly flighty creative soul who said,

"I'm making a film, want to be in it?"

"What's the money?"

"Not much."

"Well not really..."

"It's called The Futurist."

"Go on..."

"I'm making it in The Futurist on Lime Street."

"I'll do it."

It was November, cold, drizzle, dark, buses whining past with farting air brakes and misted up windows as they smooched through puddles and reflected in shops. Town had shuffled across the city towards the Liverpool One, which made me think of someone stuck in prison for a crime they didn't commit, like the Birmingham Six or something but not quite as many.

Dickie Lewis held his arm high, like he'd just slapped himself on the forehead after realising his time was nearly up and I walked down Mount Pleasant and across past the piss 'eds outside The Adelphi who hustled around cider like pigeons round crumbs.

I banged on her shutters and looked at the student flats across the way, someone was looking back and I remember they waved. I didn't wave back, which I regret now.

Bloody students.

The shutters huffed and puffed up about four feet and a head popped out underneath them,

"I can't get it up."

"We've all been there."

I ducked under the shutter, out of the rain and into the past. The foyer hadn't changed, the tiled floor, the dark walls, the ticket booth, the kiosk, the stairs off to the sides.

All the same except for the chandelier and the half ton of plaster on the floor. It was like the ceiling had given up the ghost and lent down to kiss the floor. The rain was outside but the damp was in, so damp and cold you could almost smell it. The camera lights steamed, their shadows the only straight lines left, I crunched across the floor and looked into the ticket booth, no need to lie about my age this time, there was nobody there, I'd half expected to see a skeleton with a plies of change on the counter, instead, all I saw was damp, more damp.

"Come up to the bar."

Never one to miss an opportunity I followed the torch, the floor felt crunchy, like fresh snow. I touched the wall as I climbed the stairs, regretted it, and entered the bar. It was lit by artificial light and I could hear buses, top decks just feet away through the broken glass.

"Be careful where you stand or you'll go through the floor."

I felt like Alice through the looking glass.

I looked for the silver eyelashes and found them, up close they looked even sadder, so I pulled them out of the rain and into the cold, I felt sorry for them, I cared.

The seats had gone from the auditorium, as had the bums that once sat on them. Up in the roof pigeons called to each other and I could feel rain on my face sometimes depending on where I stood. We shone torches up at the beautiful ceiling but didn't let them linger to long in case the weight of the light caused another part to fall, in one place I could see the roots of something growing in the sky, a whole new meaning to "roof garden".

One night I found a box of movie posters in a storeroom, they were rotten and crumbled if you tried to unfold them, one was for Earthquake, which was ironic, as the room looked like it had been through one.

We filmed there for four nights; I'd never been so cold and I hate to admit I was glad to leave in the end.

"Can you hold the shutter up for me?" Said one of the cameramen as he humped his gear out to the van and I obliged, straining the get it as high as I could so he could pass under without bending double. I rested the shutter on my shoulder as others took opportunity to use me as a human door stop and I remained in place for a few minutes.

It's only now I realise what it felt like that night, shutter held high, resting on my shoulder, like a jilted lovers head as I made to walk away.

The building willing me not to go, not to forget, to always hold dear.

I wish I'd left those eyelashes fluttering now; they were the only signs of life.

Here's to the future, here's to The Futurist.

36. We Deserve Better.

Do you remember when you could trust? When you could take things for granted? When if you looked at certain things they seemed solid, defined, unwavering and true?

There was a time when the pillars of Great Britain held up the country like great English Oaks, sturdy, squat, warm to the touch and everlasting. Reassuringly un-bowing in the winds of change they had stood for centuries, and would stand fast for centuries more.

If a criminal or a terrorist was released on appeal we would shake our heads and talk about "Some bad apples" or even worse "no smoke without fire" and the people wronged would get some compensation (minus the rent the Home Office took for their incarceration, which always struck me like Terry Waite paying council tax to the owner of the radiator he was handcuffed too) and go off and be bitter for the rest of their all to short lives.

I used to drink in a bar where Charles Connolly was a bouncer. Charlie had been convicted and served time for robbery in the fifties after being implicated in the notorious Cameo Cinema murders in Liverpool. This big bear of a man would once propped up a bar with me for a night telling how he had been forced by the police, by his barrister and by the prosecuting barrister to admit to something he hadn't done on pain of death. He told us how the police and prison services had abused him, worn him down and broke him on the broken wheels of justice to lie in court. And how those lies had snatched his neck from a tightening noose that claimed his co-accused, a man he'd never even met before.

That night it was hard not to believe Charlie, he rung his big bruiser hands and positively ached with honesty, but I'm afraid my doubts still remained. I'm afraid as we walked home I thought "Well you would say that wouldn't you? They wouldn't have arrested him for nothing."

Charlie died a long time ago now, I hardly knew him at all, but I wish I'd believed him that night, because now I've no doubt he was telling the truth.

I'm sorry Charlie.

Then there is Ricky Tomlinson, Jim Royle, who appears to have been abused royally by the Queens's government and judiciary. Tomlinson, convicted along with Des Warren on charges of conspiracy to intimidate. Both men were incarcerated almost as freedom fighters, wanting only the right to a fair wage and safe conditions in which to earn it, both men languished in jail, often held in solitary confinement, naked, wrapped in blankets with women folk camped outside the jail protesting their innocence. As Warren told the judge on the day of his sentencing:

"The conspiracy was between the government, the employers and the police. When was the decision taken to proceed? What instructions were issued to the police, and by whom? There was your conspiracy."

It now appears Warren was right, for his were the only honest words spoken under oath that day.

Like some banana republic our great offices of state have conspired to cover up, both for themselves and for others, be they greedy bankers, claiming MP's, fiddling Lords, kiddie fiddling priests and corrupt top cops they lived in a hall of mirrors and we trusted them, like fools.

It appears even the BBC has drawn a shell suited veil over the disgusting deeds of one of its stars, allowing him, and possibly many others, to roll like pigs in their own filth safe in the knowledge that while Auntie spoke peace unto nations, she wouldn't say squeak to Lady Justice.

How about the church? I'm almost loath to give mention to an organisation whose founder said "suffer the children".

Because suffer they did, and suffer they do, while their abusers live out pensioned retirements surrounded by a warm cocoon of conspiracy.

So we find ourselves unable to trust that and those which we held dear, George Dixon was a lie, Horace

Rumpole was a lie, George Mainwaring was a lie even Hugh Grant in Love Actually was a lie.

Justice is a word heard a lot around Liverpool of late, it's a small simple word, easy to understand, easier to implement. Truth and justice are often mentioned together like bangers and mash, fish and chips and war and peace. But unlike the others, they can't be had separately, you can't have justice without truth.

I was a policeman, I've seen people lie, seen, I once gave evidence in court about an offence I'd witnessed with my own eyes, the defendant beat his breast, frothed and flustered, rolled his eyes and sighed and the jury acquitted.

A guilty man walked, justice opened the door for him and let him pass, he was one who got away and lived to fight another day and I was upset and saddened. I couldn't look the victim in the eyes afterwards, I was ashamed and felt like a failure and I still do.

But had I lied to Lady Justice to secure a conviction, had I exaggerated and bended my story to fit onto her scales and then tipped them when she wasn't looking, I wouldn't have been able to look at myself in the eye, and I would have been more ashamed and felt more of a failure than I do.

This country, its institutions, its leaders and enforcers should feel that shame, Lady Justice should lift up her blindfold and level her sword at ones we once trusted and now doubt, lest we should start to doubt her.

We need to start again, we need truth, we need justice, we need honesty and we need to believe in it, because if we don't, we will come to expect, and accept, exactly the opposite.

And we deserve better.

Don't we?

37. The Big Daft Dog.

The big daft dog bounced and flounced into my life in 2002. My life, such as it was, was very different back then. But the big daft dog wasn't, he was the same then as he was yesterday. Age had not withered him, he still loved to play, he still loved to bounce, he still loved to flounce.

If I looked at him in a certain way he be off the couch and next to his lead reading my mind before I'd thought the thought. He knew me better than I knew myself, he knew me like a shadow knows a shape, he knew better than anyone who's ever met me, he was my best mate.

He saw the highs, he saw the lows, he saw my deepest depths and my highest highs, he knew when I needed a cuddle or when I needed to play.

The big daft dog wasn't so daft after all.

We went through a lot together; there was a time, a dark time, when we lived in a car together, long winter nights sharing a blanket. He didn't complain he just kept me warm, all he wanted was to be with me, to be my mate, and he was.

We loved the beach, he loved the sea, dancing and hopping through it, his paws buffed puppy-soft by a million granules as he ran in figure of eights, tongue lolling, the joy of ears flapping, in the only space where a big daft dog could stretch those big daft legs completely. Happy to be alive, running with his best mate... I knew how he felt.

He loved the forest, sniffing and snuffling autumn leaves, that's how we spent yesterday, walking on our secret lane, he saw a squirrel and stopped and stared then looked at me,

"Did you see that?"

I did, and I smiled, and I ruffled his ears, and he forgot all about it and got back to sniffing and snuffling.

I stopped at our bridge, and he hopped up on those big long back legs and looked over it with me, enjoying the sound of the water below, watching the silver splashes as it broke over rocks, happy to be alive.

He sat with me on the couch last night, he had a dream, a dog dream, he ran and twitched for a minute until I rested my hand on his head and scratched his big daft ear. He sighed, stretched and farted.

And I loved him, he was my big daft dog.

I hope he is still running in those dreams tonight, now that he is gone.

Goodnight Boo, I love you and I'll miss you, you big daft dog.

38. The Gates Of Hell.

When I was seventeen the gates of hell were eight feet high and made of rubber. Whenever they opened they made a noise that sounded like two whales in wetsuits on a kids slide and even now, nearly twenty five years later, whenever I hear a whale in a wetsuit on a kids slide I shudder (granted that's not very often but you get my drift).

They stood at the end of a warehouse where I'd managed to land a temporary summer job loading wagons with heavy boxes. When I say heavy, I mean really heavy, the job was both back breaking and soul destroying with long hours and tough foremen who would chivvy and chide the poor souls who had found themselves lost and abandoned in a factory in Speke from eight till six, Monday to Friday with three quarters of an hour for lunch.

It wasn't all bad though, because it was hard hot work they allowed us as many drink breaks as we wanted, unfortunately, none of us wanted them. Well that's not exactly true, we all wanted them, it is just we were too scared to take them.

Which is where the gates of hell come in.

To get to the kitchen we had to pass through the portal to Hades, and on the other side we didn't find Cerberus, what we found was much worse than that, we found about thirty to forty women, Mums, daughters, grandmothers all mix of womankind existed behind the gate, and it's only source of entertainment was the poor young men who worked "on the other side".

I remember the first time I wanted to go and get a drink, one of the foremen started laughing and said something along the lines of "Are you mad?" as I walked towards the doors. I pushed them open and saw the "packers" hunched over boxes stuffing smaller boxes into them. I was a confident young man so I don't recall any sense of trepidation as I headed towards the kitchen, I do recall seeing a few of the packers looking up as I wandered through them, I also recall one or two whistling as I went by. I filled the kettle and made some tea and then headed back to work, cup in hand unaware that the next kettle I would have to deal with was a wholly different one filled with fish.

This time when I faced the packers they were ready for me, they shouted, squeezed, pinched, pulled and petted me. I spilt my tea, flushed and blushed, pushed and pretended I wasn't scared when in truth I was. I remember feeling a hand on my crotch and the "Woooh!" echoing around the room as I pushed it away.

It was a long walk; I made it only once and swore I wouldn't do it alone again. A few of the lads I worked with that summer fared considerably worse than me, I recall one young man returning from hell sans his trousers. The wicked women of the west had held him down and debagged him, he had scratches on his legs and I recall that he was tearful in his humiliation and his underpants.

The foremen spoke to the women and asked them to calm the "joking around" down after that, they didn't. It soon even became unsafe for us to go in there in groups, we laughed about it, but we were actually rather scared, though none of us would admit it, to do so would be to invite ridicule.

Such was factory life back then, dignity in the workplace? More like indignity, but it was thirty years ago, I was an adult and I lived through it, I'll not be ringing the police, even if the Director General of BBC seems to think I should.

I listened with interest the other morning as Liz Kershaw told of being groped whilst being on air at Radio One. The next day Sandi Toksvic told the world she also had been "unpleasantly groped" whilst on air (I'm not sure there is such a thing as a "pleasant grope" but maybe I'm wrong). The media seemed to lose sight of the severity of the Savile allegations and started to navel gaze and talk about a "rugby club culture at the BBC" in the eighties, pretty much every newspaper led with the story and the DG exclaimed "anyone who suffered these assaults should contact the police immediately". Desperate to avoid criticism promises were made about internal investigations and the need for people to speak freely and instead of groped, breasts were beaten with statements about "lessons being learned."

Now I'm not downplaying these assaults, they are serious and distressing and should never be tolerated. But today it is 2012, the world is a vastly different place from the 80's. As much as we like to pretend, a great many mixed workplaces in those days were like a poorly written seventies sitcom full of lecherous men with wandering hands at Christmas parties and battle axe women who touched up young apprentices. It was wrong, but it happened, the BBC wasn't special, it was typical and the only reason we are hearing about it now is because the BBC seems intent to flagellate itself for fear of being criticised by the press over every incident that occurs there.

These are important issues but surely to discuss them in the same context as the crimes Savile is alleged to have committed is wrong? Should the BBC and its employee's not be asking why if, as Kershaw stated, Savile's behaviour was an "open secret" nobody had the guts to say something to stop it? I watched as an ex newsreader told a story about finding Savile with a young girl on his lap and his hand up her skirt, forgive me, but I was almost as angry with her as I was with him for not saying something to put a stop to this behaviour.

Time and again I've heard tell of him being an intimidating and powerful figure with people being afraid to speak out, really? You'd be more worried about your job than whether you could stop a child being raped?

Or did they think Jim would fix it for them to end up in a coffin?

I think not, I just think they were lazy and selfish, people who were paid to speak, not speaking out.

39. Secrets.

I remember the floor of my dad's shed; it had paper thin boards that were so frayed at the end you could see the flag stones twelve inches below. Most of them stopped short of each other, like rotten teeth in a gritted mouth, and I would bounce on their tips like a seven year old high diving champion who didn't have a pool to practice in.

There was one window, about two feet square, that had long been cracked and seemed to be held together by a Castrol oil sticker and dirt. It sat to the left of the bench and I never got to see the view from it because it was higher than four foot six... and I wasn't.

The outside was painted a weird shade of light green that would now be mixed for you in the diy shop by a kid covered both in spots of acne and paint or a pensioner who wanted to retire but couldn't so who recited the mantra,

"It keeps me active."

So as not to go mad.

I'm guessing my Dad mixed the paint from leftovers of the many seventies shades he'd splashed around the house in an attempt to make up for our lack of colour telly and it seemed faded before it left the brush.

Today we'd say "pastel", then they'd say "It needs another coat."

You had to lift and push the shed door and the latch never quite met the hasp due to those drooping hinges, and whenever you walked into the house from the garden my parents always said that most secure of welcomes,

"Have you locked the shed?" In a way that made me think the queen left the crown jewels in there during the week next to the boxes of mixed screws and rusty cans.

She could have, because nobody ever broke in, probably due to the tiny pad lock so small a sparrow could have forced it with a toothpick.

I used to love going in the shed, I can smell it now, it smelt of damp wood, oil and adventures. It wasn't just a shed to me though; it was a starship, a pirate ship or a prisoner of war camp.

Two foot battens of wood became swords that became rifles that became swords again, and the window I couldn't see out of became my portal to the universe from where I could see anything and anywhere.

I just had to dream.

My mates and I would assault the shed, creeping up the side of the house while some poor kid we didn't really like had to stand guard, looking the other way as we sidled up behind him and shot him with sticks, or stabbed him with sticks, depending on what century it was.

Sometimes, on rainy days, I would stand in the shed doorway, waiting for it to go off, listening to the pitter patter on the tar coated roof, enjoying the sensation of being a kid out in the rain without anyone shouting me to get in before I got wet.

I'm forty five, and I still enjoy that feeling.

Still a kid I the rain.

I'll make a confession here, one that has been a secret for over thirty five years kept between two people until now.

I broke my Dad's drill in that shed.

Or rather I broke a hair like drill bit he had in an old fashioned "bit and brace" thing that Noah must have used on the ark.

It was the end of one of those long days that were just starting to shorten as August gave way to September and my shipmates had long gone home for supper and then bed. I'd already been shouted in twice but I knew I could get away with a couple more calls before my mum came looking to drag me into the kitchen cornering me with a brick of green soap telling me to,

"Wash your face and hands." With a stinky dishcloth that was probably a pair of old knickers boiled in bleach just to make them scrape across my face even more.

I found the drill lying in an old tool box, burnished black with 3in1 oil and a million turns of the rickety handle that moved the gears that turned the bit. I held it up like Indiana Jones and inspected it like it was a rare object slowly turning the rattley handle as the temptation drill something became too much to bear.

I had to make a hole in something.

I looked around the shed and settled on drilling just one hole in the nearest thing to me, the thick wooden bench. I placed the bit against the wood and slowly turned the handle.

I can't remember if I was "doing" voices as I drilled, I probably was though; I was fond of voices and had a collection of Americans and Germans in my repertoire. I probably told people to "Stand back, I'm going in" or words to that effect. I'm guessing my little mad mind was on a journey to the centre of the earth, or maybe defusing a WW2 bomb even brain surgery wasn't out of the question, behind me I would have imagined a crowd of people straining to see while admiring my bravery or expertise.

I was enjoying myself right up until the drill bit plinked into submission and I was left with half of it stuck in the drill, and the other half sticking out the bench.

I can still remember the cold hand of fear that gripped me, the coldness at the top of my stomach like it was wide open and exposed to an arctic wind. It lasted a second before it became panic. I dropped the drill and pulled at the stub of the bit that stuck out of the bench like a stubborn weed. My fingers tried to grip the metal but hurt as they slid up the steel making me feel like an imposter at the sword and the stone. I quickly realised nothing was going to pull that bit out and grabbed a hammer, driving it into the wood with a couple of hefty two handed thumps.

Like a murderer in a mystery play I took the drill itself and secreted it behind some old timber out of sight, surveyed the scene, took a deep breath and went into the house to wash my hands.

I'm sitting here now, reading this amazed at my coolness under stress, the only conclusion I can draw is that I must have been a calculating little bastard because I managed to behave normally enough for my Mum not to become suspicious and the drill and snapped bit was never mentioned again, well, for about seven or eight years anyway.

I don't know why it came up that night all those years later, sitting with my Dad in the pub. I wasn't drunk, I didn't get drunk with my Dad. We would only have two pints and then he would go home and leave me to my mates to sort out the drunk thing.

We'd started drinking together once a week, him with his mild and me with my lager, sitting and talking, getting to know each other, him turning into to an old man, and me turning into a young man. A brief crossover when we would cease to be man and boy, and become that rarest of things... mates.

It didn't last long, he died soon after, cut short on a journey, snapped off like the drill, long before its time, hammered into some wood and buried out of sight.

I remember I told him about the drill and he just smiled and took a sip, nodded his head and smiled.

"I know." He said quietly, a man who used words like they were rationed and who spoke softly so as not to scare the next one off.

"How did you know?"

"I found the drill behind the wood where you hid it. Thanks for telling me though."

I think I laughed it off, I know I shook my head and I also know he just kept smiling and took another sip of his pint.

I'm glad I got to tell him, even though he'd known all along..

It was only a tiny thing, no big deal, a couple of pence lost down the years like change down the back of the couch forgotten about until someone shakes it. But it had bothered me, like the tiny drill itself was stuck in me like a splinter and not that old workbench.

Someone told me a secret not long back, this time it was bigger than a tale about a drill bit. This time it was story about a secret lover and the impending trauma of being found out.

The secret was crushing them the weight than a rolling ocean and dragging two families down to the depths maybe to be lost forever. They cried when they told me and I did my best "Dad" impression by letting them speak without casting judgement.

It wasn't as easy as I thought.

I advised them to "get it off your chest and come clean, you'll feel better."

They did... and they don't.

Two people jumping into bed and keeping it a secret was never going to work, and maybe it was daft of me to think telling the truth would improve matters.

Next time, maybe they should look before they leap.

40. Night Time Is The Right Time.

I discovered something about myself last night that I maybe should have realised about one thousand years ago... I'm a night time person.

Granted, like I said, I should have realised a while ago, what with the not having a proper job for the last twenty years, constantly working nights and not knowing how to work an alarm clock, all this really should have tipped me off.

But it wasn't until last night that it finally hit home.

I was booked to do an interview on the excellent John Barnes's BBC Radio Lancashire show, which runs from 10pm until 1am of a week night. It's a mix of chat, listeners calling in and music, I was there plugging my book and hopefully entertaining his audience for an hour or so.

I set off from Liverpool at about 8.45 for the forty mile drive up the M6 to Blackburn where the studio is based. A beautiful summer's day was changing into a beautiful summer's night and as I headed off toward Lancashire the sunset dribbled down the sky like a blob of orange paint on a deep blue background inching its way to the horizon before it fell off the canvas and out of sight.

Off to my right the odd star was showing its face and the motorway was clear except for night time truckers or tardy sales reps. It was one of those rare occurrences you get nowadays when you can sit back and just enjoy the drive. By the time I got to Blackburn the sun had gone to start a day shift the other side of the world and when I parked in the BBC car park the place was lit by street lamps and was empty except for a solitary curious cat and me.

Security cat let me pass and once inside the building I waited in the empty newsroom before heading to the studio, computer monitors and scraps of paper littered the room, it looked like a film set waiting for actors and I guessed it wasn't so calm during the day.

They are strange places radio stations, more so than TV stations. Nowadays on the telly we are used to seeing people behind the presenters, phones pressed to their ear, banging away on keyboards with sweaty brows and deadlines. But a radio station is like a swan in the water, we just hear the calm voice while unseen, unheard, there is a frantic paddling team of people keeping the whole thing afloat and moving forward of a day. But of a night, when the reporters have gone home, the managers have put away their calculators and the cleaners have tidied up all the paper coffee cups, something magical happens and they slow down and become your friend.

While I sat in the studio and listened to John chat to his first caller, Leah from Swinton, about Coronation Street I felt real warmth that you wouldn't get with daytime radio, an intimacy between Leah, John and the thousands of people listening around the North West. He was in their bedrooms, their sitting rooms, sharing a cup of tea with them and tucking them into bed. I felt a real privilege being invited to share that warmth and I hope I didn't let them down.

I stopped for fuel on my way home from the station, as I paid the guy at the window I heard John on the radio inside the store, keeping someone else company for the night, along with the taxi drivers, the truckers and the other late night lost souls.

As I headed back onto the M6, just me, the stars, the odd lorry lit by a lazy moon and John on the wireless, I wound down my window, rested my elbow on the frame and thought,

"I love the night time, and I love night time radio even more."

Short Stories.

Over the page I've chosen to enclose a few short stories that have been previously been on sale for the Kindle only as a little bonus in this edition of the book. The shorts are all still available separately to buy on Amazon, but come on; it would be daft to pay for them after I've left them here for you!

Hope you enjoy them Tony.

X

41. Alex And The Flowers.

Alex shook the flowers in an attempt to get the lady to take them from his hand. She stared at them a moment, then looked up and down the busy street in the heart of the business district, paused, bit her lip, and then looked back at Alex,

"Why?"

"Because I want you to be happy, I want to make you smile."

"I don't understand, why me?" she replied, the lip still bitten,

"I just picked you at random, you were walking along and I picked you. It's nothing creepy; I just want to make people smile." He shook the flowers again, "Take them, please, they are for you."

"What about my husband? What will he say when I come home with flowers from a strange guy?"

"Give them to someone else, make them happy. Just smile, be happy."

She glanced around again and then took the flowers, Alex smiled and held out his arms,

"There! See? It's easy!"

She shook her head and smiled,

"This is crazy, but..." A laugh now, "You made me happy!"

Alex bowed slightly and smiled back,

"It makes me happy to make you happy."

The girl watched him walk away, he didn't look back and she looked at the flowers and laughed to herself, fixed a few petals and glanced back at Alex who was fast disappearing into the homeward bound crowds, bustle into the hustle.

Alex walked awhile, looking at faces as they went by, he was aware that nobody looked back, he felt like a ghost, passing among them unseen.

He tried to smile at people but couldn't, tried to catch their eyes but couldn't, they pushed past him, cell phones clamped to their heads like tiny talking shields from the outside world.

Alex was alone.

He stopped and looked up at the street sign, East 40th, he'd walked a long way, swept by the tide.

Too soon to go home, too soon to sit in the silence, Alex had more to work to do, more smiles to give, he turned around and headed back to where he come from.

He stopped at the flower stall; the fat Russian guy who owned it took the skinny cigarette out of his mouth and picked some tobacco off his tongue with a dirty finger that hung out his woollen glove like a sausage in a sweater. He stared at the finger a moment and then looked up at Alex and squinted, shaking his head,

"You back again? How many times is this today?" The Russian peered out from behind the smoke of the cigarette that had found its way back to his mouth in quick time as if by magic,

"A bunch of flowers please." Alex pointed at some yellow flowers that were starting to tire after a day on the stall.

"Dis must be six or seven bunches today."

"The yellow ones, I need the yellow ones." Alex pointed again, but this time with the neatly folded ten dollar bill he was holding ready, "Please give me them, I need them."

The fat Russian put his hands on his hips and stared at Alex,

"You sure are buying a lot of flowers."

Alex waved the bill and looked everywhere but at the Russian,

"Please, the flowers, I need them."

"What are you doing with all my flowers? You better not be dumping them, that'll get me in trouble with the city."

"Please," this time Alex sounded like a child, and for a moment he felt desperate and ready to cry, "please give me the flowers."

"Give the guy the flowers for Christ's sake!" Said a hotdog guy who was stirring some onions as he watched. "The guy just wants to buy some flowers!"

The Russian took out the cigarette again and waved it at the hot dog guy,

"Not until he tells me what he's doin' with them, I wanna know where these are goin. I don't want someone comin' down here telling me I been sellin' flowers to a crazy guy all afternoon! Every day this week you been here buying my flowers, I wanna know what's going on?"

The Russian turned his back on the hot dog guy and put the cigarette back in his mouth and rolled it around his lips before folding his arms and staring at Alex, who, in turn, looked at the floor and twisted the ten dollar bill in his hands.

"Hey buddy, you wanna buy a hotdog instead of some flowers?"

Alex didn't turn to look at the hotdog guy; he frowned and twisted the note in his hands some more then looked up at the Russian through his fringe, shy, unsure.

"I give them to people."

"Seven bunches? You gave someone seven bunches? I can do you a bulk order, it'll be cheaper."

"No, I give them to different people... it... I want... I need to make them happy." Alex lowered his eyes to the floor again, embarrassed by his need.

"Hey give 'em a hotdog! That'll make them happy!"

The Russian and Alex ignored the hotdog guy, and Alex glanced back up and watched as the cigarette stopped moving and glowed bright for a second.

"You buy strangers flowers?" With a tilt of the head.

"I buy ladies flowers, to make them smile."

"You some kind of pervert?"

"No."

"Why'd you do it then?"

"To make them smile." This time with a shrug.

The Russian unfolded his arms and rubbed his stubble, he looked out of place surrounded by the beauty of the colours on his stall.

Like a gargoyle lost in a garden.

Alex flicked the ten bucks towards him, swatting at a money fly, the Russian's eyes dropped to it then back to Alex's face.

"I don't understand what you are doing."

"I'm just trying to make them happy."

"Why?"

"Give the guy the god damn flowers Ivan! Let the guy do his thing!" Hotdog guy was laughing as he put some onions on a dog for a customer.

"Why do you do it? I don't understand?" This time the Russian spoke quietly, so only Alex could hear him over the sounds of the city street.

Alex risked a glance into the eyes of the Russian before looking down again, he thought about why he did it, looked for words to explain, but they weren't there.

"I don't know I just want to make people smile."

The Russian looked past Alex at the hotdog guy and sighed, he turned and pulled down the yellow flowers Alex had asked for, wrapped them and held out his hand for the ten bucks that Alex passed across, he offered Alex the flowers but pulled them back sharply as Alex reached across.

"The last bunch, dis is the last bunch this week. If you want more flowers you better get them somewhere else. Understand?"

Alex nodded and held out his hand for the flowers, the Russian paused then passed them across,

"Thank you."

"Gerbera."

"What?"

"They ain't yellow flowers; they are called gerbera's."

"Gerbera, I'll remember."

"So will I, no more this week, you understand?"

"Yes."

"You can have as many hotdogs as you want."

Alex looked at t hotdog guy properly for the first time. Hotdog guy laughed a loud laugh and showed the world that he had a front tooth missing; Alex nodded and stepped off the kerb to cross the road. He darted in and out of the traffic, which was a slow moving mechanical glacier stop starting its way home. When he reached the other sidewalk he looked up and down the street, it was quieter now, offices had emptied and lights were coming on in the glass atriums of the shiny sky scrapers that hemmed him in. He could feel them looming, tilting close together like they were peering down on him from above. He didn't look up, he never looked up, he looked at the people's faces passing, like a mouse at the foot of a skirting board he stayed close to the buildings.

It was the only time he liked to look into people's faces, he was safe when they were hurrying, they didn't look back or lock onto his eyes. In the city he felt like one of them, in the city everyone was afraid of connections, afraid of touching, getting to know each other.

In the city he felt normal.

He walked along the street some way, holding the flowers like a flaming torch in a cave, and then he saw her. He so wanted to make her smile, she was on her cell phone, talking quickly, angry maybe, standing by the bus stop, she was tall, pretty, in a tired, ten hour day sort of way. Too long in the office had dried her skin, morning make up had given way to evening pallor. The bus pulled in and people edged to the door with shuffled steps, she was near the front and Alex had to push his way to her, she stepped up onto the bus, he could hear her,

"So what Eddie? I finished late! Quit bitchin' we can go out tomorrow!"

An old lady was in front of her, sifting through change, the girl tried to reach around her to flash her pass but the driver stared straight ahead, lost in thought.

"Eddie! Eddie! Listen to me, it's only a date! We can go to a... Eddie stop shouting at me!"

Alex stepped onto the bus and touched her elbow with the tip of his finger; she turned, angry at the intrusion of human contact in a big city. A long strand of hair fell across her face and she swiped it away with her bus pass.

"What?"

"For you, some flowers to make you smile."

"What?"

"For you."

"For me?"

"To make you smile."

The old lady looked up from her purse at them both and smiled but Alex didn't see her, he was looking at the lady on her phone who lowered it from her ear an inch or two. Alex offered the flowers again, he could hear a tiny voice coming out from the earpiece of the cell, it sounded angry.

The lady suddenly put the phone back to her ear,

"Eddie! Shut up will you? I got a crazy guy here."

Alex felt his cheeks redden and he saw the flowers lower an inch or two, even though he hadn't noticed the strength leaving his arm, or his will.

The lady half turned her head to look at the old lady and then looked at Alex from the corner of her eye,

"They are gerbera." Alex said softly.

"What are?"

"The flowers."

"Come on lady; get on the god damn bus already!" Someone shouted behind Alex but he didn't turn to look, he just shook the flowers.

The lady seemed to soften; she glanced at her cell again and then used her thumb to press a button before lowering it to her side.

"I just want you to smile."

"I don't gotta do nothing else other than smile?"

Alex nodded.

She took them and smiled, and he smiled back and stepped off the bus.

Time to go home, home to the silence, the four walls and the memory of the smiles he'd given.

42. The iHit.

Crace looked around the half empty diner and pulled the yellow nylon baseball cap he was wearing off his head and ruffled his $100 dollar haircut for the fifth time in the last hour. He sighed, looked at the cap and frowned at the smiling Mickey Mouse that was beaming up at him from above the brim and tossed it onto the table.

"You want more coffee?" it was the Filipino waitress back again,

"No."

"The boss say you gotta order food or you gotta go soon, you taking up space for eating customer." She tapped her pencil tip on the pad, like she was practicing her full stops, and put all her weight onto her left leg causing her right hip to pop out. Crace guessed her feet were hurting after working a ten hour shift in this shit hole and just under his irritation a tiny bubble of sympathy floated to the surface.

"Look, I'm waiting for someone, I can't order till they get here."

"You or Mickey gotta eat or else he say you gotta go wait somewhere else." She flicked a glance at Mickey on the table and Crace felt his sympathy bubble go "pop".

"I'll take a coffee." He said looking away from her and out the window.

"No coffee now, unless with food."

"Jesus Christ, this place is half empty, what difference does it make?"

"Boss say you wanna wait, you gotta eat, that the rule."

Crace sighed and whipped out his wallet from the back pocket of the cheap jeans he was wearing, pulled out a fifty and tossed it on the table in the vague direction of the waitress as he turned away,

"You tell the boss I just turned his shit-bird diner into a goddamned waiting room okay?"

The waitress picked up the fifty dollars and slipped it under her pad faster than a card sharp on a riverboat and smiled down a Crace, flashing her tiny white teeth at him for the first time since he'd been there.

"You want coffee now?"

"Fuck off."

Evening was sauntering past outside and pretty much had the street to itself. The Lower Manhattan winter hadn't quite blown in yet and a few of the tooth pick trees still had some leaves clinging on for dear life. It was starting to rain and Crace wished he'd been allowed to drive across town instead of having to get the bus, he decided to get a cab home and mentally promised himself a drink of something strong as soon as he made it back to the apartment, unless that bitch was still there, if she was home he'd go to a bar. That was the plan until he remembered what he was wearing, he looked down at the "I love New York" tee shirt and ten dollar jeans he'd been given to wear, next to him in the window booth lay the Planet Hollywood jacket. At least he'd be able to ditch the baseball cap soon. He stared at Mickey again and longed for his usual uniform of designer brands and smart suits and wondered if he'd be too late to stop at a shop to pick up something decent to wear on his way back across town.

Crace picked up his mug and felt its chill in the palm of his hand,

"Can I get some warm coffee here?" he shouted holding up the mug like it was a flaming torch in a cave. The waitress glanced up from her magazine by the register and nodded,

"It brewing Mickey, be there soon."

Crace cursed and let mug bang onto the table making little effort to hide his irritation, fifty bucks for four cups of shit coffee, he felt like killing this bitch as well.

"Ten more minutes and I'm outta here." He whispered softly to nobody and turned back to the window to look at the rain that was now falling fast and hard, only a solitary pigeon stood in the road, looking like it had missed its bus and was waiting for a taxi.

"I know how you feel buddy." Crace said to the pigeon through the glass and turned back to shout at the waitress again. He nearly jumped out of the ill fitting jeans when he saw a man sitting opposite him in the booth. Crace took a deep breath to calm his beating heart and placed both his hands palm down on the table in front of him, just like he had been told to do in the email.

The man tilted his head slightly and looked down at the Mickey Mouse baseball cap on the table and then back at Crace,

"I felt like an asshole wearing it, I had to take it off."

The man reached under the table and then produced an iPad from somewhere Crace couldn't see, he wondered if the iPad had been taped to the bottom of the table as he noticed some marks on the back of the case as the man held it towards himself so that Crace couldn't see the screen.

Crace took the few moments to study the man sitting opposite him; he guessed the guy was about forty something, white, slim, maybe worked outside judging by the way his skin was weathered. The guy was wearing an old black leather suit jacket that looked maybe a size too big for him, it looked kind of cool on the guy and Crace liked it. He wondered if it was really old, or maybe one of those jackets that cost thousands to make them look like they cost fifty bucks. He decided to ask the guy after they'd finished their meeting.

The guy finished what he was doing with the iPad and then placed it down on the table between them. On the screen Crace could see about ten white squares on a black background. The man touched one of the squares and it zoomed in to show that there was writing on it, Crace leant forward and read the caption,

"*Put the cap on.*"

Crace looked up from the screen at the man,

"What? Are you speaking to me through the iPad?"

The man tapped the screen again,

"*Yes.*"

"Why? That's crazy, nobody can hear us."

Another tap

"*The restaurant may be bugged, you may be wired or we might be being filmed.*"

Crace looked around the restaurant nervously and then back at the man,

"I followed all of your instructions, to the letter. Nobody knows we are here I promise."

"Put the cap on."

Crace picked up the cap and pulled it on; this time he didn't care he looked a dick. He didn't care because he was too scared to care.

Another swipe,

"Hands."

Crace placed his hands back down on the table in front of him palms down and stared at the man while he played basket ball with his Adams apple. The man stared back and Crace was about to speak again when the waitress suddenly leant in and poured some coffee, Crace nearly screamed.

"Fresh coffee, you order now?"

"No, not yet, in a minute I promise."

"Hey, that iPad, they nice things, my boy want one for Christmas, too expensive for waitress though, not make enough tip."

The man opposite smiled at her and placed his hand over the top of the cup she had put down for him and shook his head slightly. She smiled back, glad that this new guy wasn't as much of an asshole as the one who had been here for an hour and turned away saying,

"I be back soon take order."

Crace looked at his coffee but didn't pick it up, the email he'd received setting up the meeting had expressly told him to keep his hands palms down on the table at all times, it was the same one that had told him the locker number where he had found the bag with the dumb clothes he was wearing, the clothes and the hat. That fucking hat.

"I feel dumb in this hat, I look like a redneck." The man tilted his head again and Crace suddenly realised he might just have insulted him, he fought to take control of that bouncing Adams apple and made an attempt at swallowing it and an apology, "I'm sorry, not that there is anything wrong with being a redneck, it's just it isn't my style, you know?"

The man tapped the screen,

"I needed you to stand out in the crowd."

"You followed me?"

"Yes."

"All the way over?"

"Yes."

"You know where I live?"

"Yes."

"Jesus."

They stared at each other across the table for a moment, and Crace puffed out his cheeks and nodded to his coffee,

"Can I take a drink?"

The man nodded and Crace picked up the mug, careful to keep his other hand down on the table top. The coffee warmed his throat and cooled his nerves so that when he put the mug back down he felt a little bit more in control.

"Have you got the answer to every question I am going to ask programmed into that thing?"

"No."

"Well we've got a problem if I ask one it can't answer haven't we?"

"No."

Crace smiled in spite of himself and took another sip of coffee, he glanced around the diner and noticed there was now only about six or other customers in there, most of them with heads buried in meals or conversations. The man had chosen the venue well.

"Okay, let's get down to business here; I gotta get back across town. This is what I want you to do..."

The man held up the palm of his right hand and with his left index finger tapped at a square on the screen, Crace leant forward to read it.

"You have asked me to kill your wife; I will do this for fifteen thousand dollars. Half at the end of this meeting and half after I have completed the task. The figure is non-negotiable as I explained in our previous correspondence. The manner of the task will be to my choosing. The collection of the outstanding monies will be to my choosing. If you do not pay the outstanding amount I will kill your parents in New Hampshire. If you speak to anyone of this matter I will kill your sister in Georgia. Once I have killed these people I will find you and kill you. If you behave in the manner I have told you and follow all of my instructions, at the completion of the matter you will never see me again. Is this understood?"

Crace sat back and let his mouth hang open for a moment while his brain figured out how to close it, a moment passed until he found some words.

"How did you know about my folks and my sister?"

The man tapped the screen again summoning another caption,

"Answer yes or no."

"There won't be a problem with the money or the job I promise."

"Answer yes or no."

"Yes."

Crace leant back from the table and stared at the man who coolly stared right back at him. Prior to the meeting Crace had wondered if this guy was just some sort of nut job fantasist who was pretending to be a hit man, but right now, looking across the table at this guy, he felt like he was staring at death.

Death stared back, smiled and nodded, as if reading Crace's mind. The man tapped another white box and Crace leant forward to read it,

"If you wish to leave now you may do. We will never see each other or speak again and you will be safe to carry on with your life as if this meeting had never taken place. You have ten seconds to get up and leave the table."

"I don't want to leave, I need... no, I want to do this I swear." Crace whispered urgently, leaning in close, head inches from the table, the light of the iPad illuminating his face from below. The man didn't reply, and it took Crace a moment to realise death was tapping his index finger on the table.

He watched it. Eight, nine, ten, before the finger pressed another square on the iPad,

"You want me to execute your wife, Karen, who works as a lawyer Maybrick Legal Inc. You want me to do this so that you can inherit Karen's wealth, wealth that was left to her by her father who died last year, and also a joint six million dollar insurance policy that is payable should either of you die before your apartment is paid for. Is this correct?"

"Jesus, it sounds like I am one evil son of a bitch, but let me tell you buddy, she is looking to nail my ass to the wall if the divorce she is threatening me with goes though. I'm in a hole here, I gotta girlfriend who is pushing me to move in with her, my job is up and down, it ain't easy being a broker these days I gotta tell you. I can't afford to split from that bitch and get a divorce."

"Answer yes or no."

"Yes. Jesus Christ! It's correct. Yes."

"If you wish to leave now you may do. We will never see each other or speak again and you will be safe to carry on with your life as if this meeting had never taken place. You have ten seconds to get up and leave the table."

This time Crace counted along with the tapping finger, eight nine ten. He didn't leave; he just sat with his hands on the table like the first email had told him too.

"You are about to contract me to kill your wife Karen. You must place the first fifteen thousand dollars, as

instructed, in a brown paper parcel, in used one hundred dollar bills onto the table. Once I pick up the money the deal is final with no provision for alteration or cancelation. Do you understand? Yes or No?"

Crace licked his lips and then chewed the bottom one, this was it, at last he was out of it and now his heart beat a little faster in excitement. There was no way this could come back on him, he'd been careful to cover his tracks with this, there was no way any of it could be traced, all he had to do was look surprised when the cops told him Karen was dead, he'd been acting all his life, one more little scene would be easy to play.

"Yes." He reached into the Planet Hollywood jacket and took out the fifteen thousand and placed it on the table next to the iPad. The man stared back at him for a moment and then tapped the screen again.

"If you wish to leave now you may do. We will never see each other or speak again and you will be safe to carry on with your life as if this meeting had never taken place. You have ten seconds to get up and leave the table."

Crace shook his head at the guy to let him know he was in, committed to this. It felt like he'd just done a deal on the stock exchange, that feeling he got when he knew he'd made the right decision and struck a home run.

"Keep counting buddy, I ain't going anywhere."

Eight... nine...ten.

The man smiled and nodded, picked up the money and placed it into his pocket, this reminded Crace to mention the jacket before the guy left, deciding 30k granted him at least one question.

He watched as the man put the iPad to sleep and pick it up with his right hand and then noticed the man's left hand as it pulled a silenced Glock 9mm pistol out from under the leather. Crace watched the matt black silencer slide out from inside the jacket like a mamba from under a rock and realised the coat had been too big so as to hide the gun.

The pistol clicked once, although Crace never heard it, due to him already pretty much being dead. His head made more noise than the gun as it landed face first onto the hands he had been instructed to place in front of him. Had he been able to take a look he would have seen that Mickey had been gut shot and was leaking brains all over the table.

The man stood up, and walked out of the diner with the pistol back under his jacket. He smiled at the waitress, who was straining to see where that awkward bastard with the dumb cap had gone over the high back of the booth,

"You come again soon now."

The man nodded, left the diner and walked two blocks before he heard the sirens. He climbed into the rental car and smiled at Karen.

"Did he want me dead? Did he?"

"Yes."

"That son of a bitch... did you... did you do it?"

"Yes."

"Oh my god, I can't believe it."

Karen sat for a moment with her hand over her mouth, the shock hitting home almost as hard as the bullet that had been meant for her. They sat in silence watching the blue and red flashing lights down the street bouncing off the rain and buildings. The windows were starting to steam and so where Karen's eyes. She suddenly remembered their deal and reached for her handbag.

"I'm sorry I almost forgot. Here, it's your money."

She held up a brown package and then man shook his head and held up the iPad again for her to see,

"He's paid for it."

Karen watched as the man got out of the car and walked to the nearby subway, he disappeared from view down the steps and she never saw him again.

Just like the iPad had said.

43. The Droppers.

"It isn't the jumping that's the problem, it's the landing." That's what my first sergeant told me back when I was a fresh out the box beat cop over in Brooklyn about twelve years back, it must have been around 2014, around autumn time, just as it was getting cool.

After the summer.

The first of the jumping had just started; a trickle was slowly turning into a flood. We didn't call them droppers back then either; we still called them suicides, maybe because back then we cared. Now? Well now I guess we are just sick and tired of scraping them up.

I stared up at the ledge above where the latest dropper lay at my feet, same as usual; it was just a ledge with no sign of the drama that played out on its edge minutes before. A pigeon stared back down at me and I wondered if it had witnessed this guy trying to fly, shaking its head at the dumb human jumping off with no wings.

We might be dumb, but at least we don't eat fries off the floor.

It was getting hot as the morning sun came of age and I started regretting not leaving my jacket in the car, the guy who owned the shop where the dropper had landed glared through the glare that was bouncing off the glass door. I watched as he pulled a face and tapped his finger on his watch and then held out his hands pleading to me. He wanted to open. And having a dead flat guy as a welcome mat wasn't good for business. I signalled back and mouthed "fifteen minutes" and the shop keeper threw up his hands and disappeared back into the darkness of the air cooled store.

I crouched down next to the dropper and looked at the back of his head, he'd landed face down. It was getting close to the moment when we had to roll him over and check his pockets, the worst time.

"Is he dead?" Detective Larry Flynn squatted down opposite me and took a drink from his coffee and waved a bag of donuts in my direction.

"Ask him." I replied, shaking my head both at the donuts and my partner.

Larry had been shot in the throat years ago, it made him sound like he was always out of breath when he spoke. I liked Larry but I didn't like donuts, I figured most cops ate them because they thought they should, not 'cos they liked them. They made my fingers sticky and teeth feel like they were made of sugar, so I just stuck to health food of a day, and bourbon of a night.

The bourbon took the taste of the health food, and the day, away.

"You been up to look at where he come from?" Larry squinted up, using the donut bag as a sunshade. I figured the pigeon was looking down with a little more interest now.

"Not yet, you wanna wait here with the dropper till the city come get him?"

"Yeah, I'll follow you up."

I left Larry and the dropper and went into the building. It was cool in the lobby as I jabbed the button for the noisy old lift that sounded like a freight train falling down a drain pipe. When it finally rattled into sight an old Chinese lady stared at me through the iron grill waiting for me to open it. She was carrying a little yellow dog that had eyes like blood shot pool balls covered in cataracts. I opened the grill, careful not to catch my finger in it, or the dog, and stepped back to let her pass.

"You a cop?" She asked me, the dog sniffing what it couldn't see.

"I am."

"You here for Mickey?"

"I don't know. Who's Mickey?"

"He the dead guy outside stupid, you not see him?"

You gotta love New York and its respect for the boys in blue.

"Is that his name?"

"It was."

"Did you know him well?"

"He used to say 'Hello' when he pass by, we just neighbour, not friend."

"When did you last see him?"

"Today."

"Did he speak to you?"

"No."

"Why?"

"He was going too fast. He went past my window, he might have waved but I didn't see."

I realised I liked this crazy old lady, I guessed Mickey had too.

"When you last spoke did he mention he was feeling sad? Did he seem strange?"

"Everyone sad and strange in this city."

She stepped past me and took the dog out into the sunlight, I watched her walk past Mickey without looking down and without saying "Hello."

When I got up to Mickey's room a young beat cop was standing by the busted in door, he straightened up as I stepped out of the elevator and pushed his cap back onto his head. Trying to look like he'd seen all this before, maybe he had, I didn't care.

"You searched the apartment?"

"No sir, nobody come out or gone in since I got here."

He puffed out his chest and I figured he hadn't seen it all before.

"You can go down and help Detective Flynn search the body."

He nodded but didn't risk speaking, he knew he was doing the "turnover" and wasn't looking forward to it. Maybe the kid had seen it before after all, or maybe he'd just dreamed about it, I know I do, every god damn night the bourbon sweats out of me.

I walked into the apartment and looked at the net curtain that hung next to the open window where Mickey had left the building. It was hot in there and I put my hand on a radiator just to see if it was on, it wasn't. It felt cool and I left my hand there a moment while I looked around, chilling my blood.

It was a nice place, small but tidy. Mickey lived a clean life, not weird clean, just normal clean. In the sink I could see maybe three dishes and a pan, two days washing up, the luxury that came with living alone.

There was some mail on the table, a couple of bills, nothing too much. He had a stereo with some old vinyl; I flicked through some albums, nothing crazy there either.

Heavy metal didn't make this guy jump, not even Van Halen.

I went into the tiny bedroom; thin cotton sheets lay at the bottom of the bed like they had been kicked off in the night. An electric fan sat on the floor, it was still switched on and it looked around the room humming away, pushing the warm air as it went, losing the battle but not giving up. I liked its style because I knew how it felt. I switched it off and checked the bathroom, tooth brush, toothpaste, shower gel and towel.

Just a normal guy.

A normal dead guy.

I went into the living room and sat in the old leather armchair in front of the TV, I could see myself in the reflection, like I was in a really dark movie... Maybe I was, it sure felt like it sometimes.

I stared back at the window and sighed, it was the part I hated the most, the looking out, the looking down, the seeing what the dropper saw before they gave up fighting and threw in the towel.

I sighed, went to the window and stuck my head out. Looking down I could see them steam cleaning the pavement, Mickey had gone, turned tagged and bagged. On his way to the morgue to be filed and piled with all the other days droppers.

I looked along the ledge to where he must have sat before he went; there was nothing, no clue, no pigeon, no Mickey. Just an empty space like the empty space he jumped out into. I looked down again and then ducked back into the apartment, out of the sun, away from the ledge.

I heard a knock and went to the door and pulled it open, it was the building superintendent. A little old guy with a torn sweater, a hat, a bag of tools and some body odour.

"I gotta fix the door." He pointed at the broken frame and I nodded and turned away. If I couldn't find answers I was going to find relatives, I just hoped they lived far away so I didn't have to use my sad face when I told them that their beloved Mickey hadn't learned to fly.

Behind me I heard the snap of a tape measure and the scrape of a chisel, I glanced at the old man who had put on a pair of half round glasses and was staring at the door frame as he worked. He looked up at me and smiled and then pushed back his hat with a stubby brown pencil in stubby brown hand.

"I'm getting good at this; this is the fifth time in a year now."

I nodded.

"I even buy timber special, I store it out back."

I leafed through some mail.

"These kids, they give up. There is nothing here for them, nothing for them to look forward to. They watch the news, they read the internet, they hear, day after day and night after night people telling them how things are bad and how things ain't getting better and they give up."

I looked up at the old man again; he was back looking at the door jamb, face inches away from it as he squinted over the glasses, taking away the splintered wood. He didn't look up from his work as he spoke.

"You see, this is why they always told us suicide is a sin, when I was a kid I'd be in church and they would slip it in every now and then, "You ain't going to heaven if you kill yourself". So we didn't, we didn't want to go to hell see? But now, the kids they figured out there ain't no hell to be scared off, they figured out the only thing when you die is an end to your problems. Soon as they see they're just gonna be a normal person they don't see the point of carrying on. Who wants to be normal?"

The old man finally looked up at me and shrugged, and I shrugged back just before he set back to chiselling.

"Kids wanna be rock stars, they wanna by movie stars, they wanna have money and dames. But when they realise they ain't gettin' none of that they don't wanna work in insurance, or be a building superintendent. So they just call it a day and punch out. That's why so many of them are doing it; it's easy, once you push off out the window gravity makes up your mind real quick. When it's done it's done. Just blackness and you weren't never here 'cept for some bills and a crummy apartment you were paying too much for anyway."

I shook my head at the old man as he measured the door frame again and then stuffed the chisel in the bag. He nodded to me and headed off to get some timber.

I looked at the letters in my hand and then at the window. Dust floated in the sun's rays and I found myself staring at the tiny flecks, drifting through the light, going nowhere... slowly.

44. Coal On The Windowsill.

I know a girl who keeps a piece of coal on her windowsill.

It's just an old lump of coal that was found on a beach, it's almost smooth. It's fortunate that unlike us, who get lined over the years, it has shed its rough edges on its journey and now only bears the finest of scars to let you know where it's been.

If you lick your finger and rub the coal it looks shiny and new for a while but then quickly goes dull again. Like it's embarrassed to be pretty.

The coal was found while walking a big daft dog, in the rain. Some people would say that was a big daft thing to do, to go walking on a beach in the rain. But the dog didn't mind and neither did the girl.

Sometimes the rain makes things special, some places look nicer with a grey sky and mist in the distance, and the beaches of Merseyside always benefit from a filter on the lens to hide the dead seagulls and summertime beer can carnage.

And that day, the day that the coal, the dog and the girl met was one of those days.

Foggy and rain shrouded windmills waved in the distance like aliens drowning in The War Of The Worlds, the tide was so far out it looked like god had tipped the Earth on its side to look for his keys and then forgotten to put it back when he remembered where he last had them. Forlorn seagulls stood staring out to sea wondering what they had said to offend it so, like jilted lovers under the station clock in a black and white film.

The girl and the big daft dog pushed on through the rain, the dog would have followed her anywhere, he was in love after she had bought him a blue bone to squeak and fetch.

He danced around her splashing through sandy puddles and tiny rivers. His feet wet and smooth, the pavements hardness cured by the touch of the sand, polished like the coal and made smooth like a puppies, the puppy he had become again for the day.

A big daft dog and a beach are made for each other, had it been a dog that took the evolutionary step and crawled out of the water all those millennia ago we would never have evolved beyond that. A species destined to spend its existence running backwards and forwards and barking at birds.

She wondered if that would have been a bad thing?

The big daft dog and the girl stopped a while and stared out to sea, both blinking as the wind pushed tears into their eyes and then onto their cheeks, they watched as a ferry headed away from the land, no doubt onboard someone stared back, through a double glazed air conditioned window shaking their head as they cradled their glass

"Look at that girl and that big daft dog, they must be soaking"

At the girls feet lay the piece of coal, staring up, waiting to be found. Untouched by human hand until the moment that she bent down and showed it to the big daft dog... who waited for it to be thrown, but she held it, studied it, rubbed off the excess sand and sniffed it... it smelt of the sea and of memories.

She normally wouldn't pick things off the ground, the words of her mother telling her she didn't know where they had been echoed down the years and caused her to wipe her hand against her jacket sleeve and study her palm for signs of dirt.

All she saw was a few grains of straggling sand and she clapped her hands together like a percussionist who had forgotten his cymbals.

The big daft dog looked at her for a moment, tilting his head, confused at the clapping sound, in sympathy he shook himself in a vain attempt to dry off the still falling rain, took a moment to stare back at the ferry and then dashed off again, chasing something she couldn't see.

She smiled, just, and put her hands back into her pockets, balling her fist around the coal.

"We are all chasing something we can't see."

She said, softly to herself, surprised at the sound of her own voice, she glanced around but there was no one to hear her... again.

She started to walk again, following the line of the sea, further away from home, following the big daft dog.

She squeezed the coal tightly, enjoying its strength, something so small being so tough made her feel better.

She noticed the big daft dog had stopped, he was watching something behind her, she turned to follow his gaze and saw the tall guy, she hadn't seen him in weeks, she hadn't been there in weeks.

Big daft dog wandered over, he stood close to her leg, after a moment he leant against it, she felt his wet fur through her jeans and gave a little shiver as they both watched the tall guy get closer.

The tall guy waved and she moved her hand, still inside her pocket, back to him. It made her coat look like bats wing and she regretted not taking it out and waving properly.

She turned and started to walk again, big daft dog didn't run off this time, he held steady, a couple of feet away, glancing back at the tall guy every now and then.

"I didn't want to see him today."

Big daft dog glanced at her then the sea then the tall guy.

"Not today dog, why today?"

Big daft dog didn't answer. He was a dog.

"Hey! Slow down!"

She turned and the tall guy was jogging towards her,

"I was shouting, didn't you hear me?"

"The wind/"

"Yeah." he looked around, like he'd only just noticed he was outside. "It's pretty awful today."

The girl didn't answer, she took her hand out of her pocket and pulled some hair from her face, looked at the sea and then back at the tall guy, managing a thin smile.

"How are you big daft dog?" The tall guy bent down to the big daft dog who wagged his stumpy tail and bowed down on his front paws playfully. "I've not seen you for a while."

The girl didn't know who the tall guy was talking to until he turned to her.

"I was worried."

"Worried?"

"Yeah," the tall guy turned back to the dog and ruffled his ears, "last time I saw you, you seemed... upset."

This time the girl knew he was talking to her; he didn't need to look at her for her to know. She shrugged, even though the tall guy wasn't looking at her.

"I was worried." He turned as he spoke and this time she shrugged and he watched "I'm sorry, it's nothing to do with me, I shouldn't have mentioned it."

He stood up from the big daft dog and smiled; the big daft dog sniffed his leg and watched the girl.

She stared at the big daft dogs eyes, they looked worried, she wondered if hers did.

"Tough day." Was the best she could come up with.

The tall guy nodded,

"Yeah, it gets to you sometimes. Do you know something?" His turn to smile and look out to the sea "We've chatted here for months and I still don't know your name?"

He turned back to her and smiled, embarrassed, she knew what had just happened and that this was the moment she'd also known was coming, like it always came.

The tall guy waited, his smile fading slowly, like the sun behind the horizon.

The girl knew he was a nice guy, he was handsome, dressed well, she liked the way he walked on his own on the beach. He didn't need a big daft dog as an excuse to walk nowhere.

And she'd known that he was going to ask, eventually.

She shrugged again, the smile thinner than before, she flicked at the strand of hair and wished she'd worn her hat. The green woollen one that made her head look like a roll on deodorant.

The girl wished he would stop digging, to save them both embarrassment, but he didn't, he ploughed on, like the waves against the shore just to her left.

"Do you have a name?" His smile was just dipping below the horizon, if it wasn't so cold he would have blushed. "I'm Pete.,"

She smiled and nodded her head, the tall guy, held out his hand, and big daft dog moved closer, so close the girl thought, for a moment he was going to jump up and bite it.

"It's just a name, I won't stalk you to death!" Hollow laugh. "I just thought... well you know..."

She did know, but didn't want to, she was cold now, and sorry she had chose today to come back outside, maybe in a week's time she would have shook his hand, told him her name and they might have gone for coffee, swopped numbers, laughed, linked arms and walked along the beach to nowhere together.

But not now, now was too soon.

Her skin was too thin for names and coffee and linked arms. Her voice was too reedy for laughing and chatting and whispering nothings.

She was as fragile as one of the paper thin shells that dotted the beach when the tide went out.

It was too soon.

She shrugged and watched the tall guy put his hand back into his pocket; he tilted his head like the big daft dog and then looked at the sand as if he'd dropped something.

"I'd better... erm, you know?"

Said the tall guy, flicking his head to show he'd best be going, the girl looked at her feet, and when she looked up he had already turned and was leaving.

"See you soon big daft dog," he said, the big daft dog didn't answer because he was a dog, "see you soon girl on the beach."

She didn't answer either, she waved, hand in pocket, to his back, because she was scared.

She clutched the lump of coal tight again, felt its strength, and turned for home.

On the way she took it out and looked at it and smelt it again, it still smelt of the sea and of memories.

And for that reason it ended up in her pocket and then on her windowsill.

45. The Appointment.

Chris Doolen had felt like death all morning. His head hurt, his chest hurt, he kept getting pains in his left arm and he'd had to go to the toilet twice to be sick.

Chris Doolen felt like death.

He rested both elbows on his glass desk and then placed his face into his upturned palms and let out a deep sigh,

"Baby come home... please."

"I can't." His voice barely made it out of his hands and Laura, who was fourteen miles away, barely heard him.

"I can't hear you baby, speak up."

Chris raised his head and looked at the speaker phone,

"I can't, I've got too much to do here and you know I can't take time off, it sends out the wrong signal."

"You are no good to them if you are dead." Laura sounded chippy this time, she used the same voice as she had used that morning when Chris had woke up and insisted he leave even though he'd felt so bad.

"It's just a little flu, I sent Kate out to get me some hot lemon. I swear, as soon as I'm finished here I'll come straight home."

"Do you promise?" Soft voice again.

"I promise."

"Okay, if you aren't home by three I'm not speaking to tonight you okay?"

"I will be, I promise."

"I love you."

"Speak to you later." Chris risked balancing his head on one hand as he ended the call and then quickly put it back into both hands and closed his eyes.

"Er, Mr Dolan?"

Chris snapped his head up embarrassed that someone had caught him looking so fragile. At his office door was a skinny guy, maybe six foot five, he was wearing tee shirt and jeans, which wasn't unusual, Chris had worked in advertising for thirty five years and he often thought he was the last guy left who wore a suit to work in the industry. The skinny guy was still holding the door open with the longest of thin arms he'd ever seen. It was almost as if the guy had no muscle at all, just skin and bones topped off with a head that looked a little bit bigger than it should have been.

"Doolen, my name is Doolen. Can I help you?"

The skinny guy let go of the eight foot solid wood door and let it swing silently closed behind him.

"Doolen? I've got Dolan down here, ummm, it is Chris though, yeah?" Skinny guy was looking at an iPhone as he spoke, as if he was reading Chris's name off it. He suddenly looked up and smiled and Chris wondered if he was a model who was due for a casting, he had that sort of look fashion magazines liked, handsome and ugly all at the same time.

"Yeah, Chris Doolen, how can I help?"

The skinny guy un-slung a man-bag off his shoulder as he walked across to the desk and pulled out what looked like a brand new Macbook Air, he started to open it and then suddenly stopped and looked at Chris before nodding to a space on the glass desk.

"Do you mind? This will only take a minute."

"Go ahead." Chris waved his hand and pulled back some of his own papers to make a space for the skinny guy who smiled again and plopped the laptop down and pulled over a chair. He dragged it across the floor making its feet squeal on the tiles like a pig going to an abattoir.

Skinny guy sat down and pulled open the laptop and frowned.

"We only just got these things so this might take me a minute." He spoke to the screen instead of Chris and clenched his fists over the keyboard with only one index finger loose and ready to type. "I preferred the old parchment and quill myself, but technology marches on, whether we like it or not." This time he smiled at Chris and then looked back down at the screen and stuck his tongue out of the corner of his mouth as he waited for whatever the laptop was supposed to be doing to do it.

"You need to boot it up, top right corner." Chris tried to reach across the big desk but the skinny guy beat him to it and prodded the button with that loose finger and smiled again.

"I'm such an idiot, this is one of the reasons I'm running so late, they bring in these things to speed you up but they end up slowing you down."

Chris glanced at the door of his office and regretted asking Kate to step out for the hot lemon, for all her faults she would have stopped this guy walking right in off the street.

"Umm I'm a little busy here; maybe you should wait for my secretary to come back?"

"Just a second," Skinny guy pushed the pad a couple of times then looked up and smiled again, "it's you I need to see." Before looking back down to the screen which now lit his face and highlighted his sharp features like bare cliffs at sunrise.

"It's just I don't normally see people without an appointment and..."

"No, I've got your appointment right here," that smile again, "if I can find it."

"I've got an appointment with you?" Chris replied.

"Uh huh." The tongue came out again as the finger did some more prodding.

"It doesn't work like that; you make the appointment with me when you come here, well not with me, with Kate, she should be back soon so..."

"Got it! Here you are, Chris Dolan! Can you confirm your date of birth please?"

The skinny guy looked up and Chris forgot his headache and stared back and then shook his head.

"No, I can't. I'm not just going to tell you my date of birth; I don't even know who you are."

"Oh god I'm sorry! I didn't introduce myself did I? I'm sorry!" Skinny slapped his forehead and then held out the same hand again this time to shake. "I'm death."

"Excuse me?" Chris didn't make to shake the hand that waited for him hovering over the table.

"Death... I'm Death." Skinny guy waved the hand up and down an inch or two and when Chris didn't take it he withdrew and went back to looking at the screen. "I'm going to need that date of birth please Chris."

Chris looked at the guy and then back at the door before reaching for his office phone, the skinny guy looked up from the laptop and smiled as Chris picked up the phone and pressed zero before placing it to his ear.

"I'm sorry but I'm going to have security ask you to leave, if this is a joke or if you are trying to get a job here in some original way, I've got to tell you, today isn't the day."

The skinny guy smiled again, glanced at the screen and then looked at the oversize watch on his wrist that hung like a ring on a stork's leg.

"Chris I need to be moving on here, I'm already running late, which is why I've had to disturb you at work. There was a drone strike in Pakistan, hit a wedding, nightmare up there I gotta tell you. No signal and you can forget about wifi. This is what they don't understand when they bring in these things." The skinny guy lifted the laptop half an inch off the desk and then set it down again.

Chris realised the phone was dead and placed it back into its holder before looking at the skinny guy, he rubbed his left arm, even though it wasn't hurting and then tried to stand up from the desk.

He couldn't.

He rested his hands on the arms of his chair and tried to push with them but couldn't, he kicked his legs a bit and they moved but wouldn't let him stand up. He glanced under the desk then tried to push his chair back.

He couldn't.

Slowly he looked up at the skinny guy who smiled kindly and gave a half nod.

"I'm going to need you to confirm your date of birth please Chris."

"What if I don't give it?"

"Either way you are coming with me man, this just saves a lot of messing around later on."

Chris tried his legs again, pushing and twisting them but he was still unable to stand up.

"Chris?" Chris looked up at the skinny guy, "I need your date of birth?" This time with a tilt of the head.

"Fourteenth of June, nineteen sixty one."

"There you go! Thank you!" The skinny looked down to the screen as Chris picked up the phone again and listened, it was still dead, not even a hiss of static or a click when he pressed a button. He took his mobile from his shirt pocket and pressed the green button. He knew Laura would be the last call he'd made and his heart leapt as he saw "Calling Laura" fill the screen.

But that is all it did, her name filled the screen like it filled his heart but the call didn't connect, it just flashed on and off, rhythmic like the pounding he could now feel in his chest. He turned his head to look out at the floor to ceiling window that seemed to hold up the roof above.

The streets below his office were frozen, nobody moved, cars with indicators stuck on sat at red traffic lights and people stood silently mid step, waiting to carry on with their lives as soon as he was finished with his.

Only a solitary pigeon sat on his window ledge, head bobbing black eyes staring at him.

"The pigeon..." Was all he could think of to say before it flew off into the frozen sky, he watched it go up and away out of sight.

"Hmm?" The skinny guy looked up from the laptop at Chris.

"The pigeon. It flew off."

"I know, it's crazy isn't it? I don't know what it is but the 'whole time stopped still' thing never seems to bother them."

"Why?"

"God knows. Hey maybe you can ask him?" Skinny guy chuckled at the joke as he went back to looking at the screen.

Chris looked back out of the window and thought he might cry, he looked back at his phone and saw it still flashing "Calling Laura" and then looked back at the skinny guy who glanced up and smiled.

"I'm sorry this is taking so long, it's kind of unprofessional of me, I'm sorry."

Chris waved a hand as if it was nothing and looked back at the screen of the phone, he thought a while and then looked up,

"Maybe you can come back later?"

"Nice try amigo." Skinny guy smiled back and then scratched his chin, "Erm do you know how to right click on these things?"

"Push the right side of the pad."

Skinny guy sighed and leant back in the chair,

"I'm such an idiot! I'm sorry, I knew that. We have to use all this Apple stuff now, since Jobs got up there, Jesus that guy can sell. Everything has switched over and I've got to be honest, I'm not sure it is a good idea, not without some proper training anyway."

"Yeah, you should speak to someone about that."

"Oh we have, but you know what it is like, someone probably got a nice little back hander for all this, so it is pointless moaning, as soon as I get used to it something else will come along."

He smiled at Chris who noticed for the first time how big his teeth were.

"I never thought it would be like this, you know... dying..."

"It normally isn't, I am all over the place today. Did I tell you about the drone strike?"

"Uh yeah."

"Well it's thrown me right out, I'm going to warn you, you will probably have quite a wait when we are done down here. Things are pretty crazy up there."

"Well I guess I'm not going anywhere."

"You hope." The skinny guy pointed down to the floor and then smiled and shook his head. "I'm only joking, don't panic, the whole hell thing was just a put on. It doesn't exist."

"But, you mean?"

"What Hitler and Stalin and all those guys?"

"Yeah."

"They are up there man, they are kind of weird an all, but they are up there. Hitler works in the laundry. He's a funny guy when you get to know him, did you ever see that film where he does the little dance?"

"I... erm...I think so..."

"Ask him, he'll do it for you, it's hilarious, he does a little song when he does it, it's crazy with that funny accent."

"How did they get up there?"

"Same as you man, it's what I do. Although back then it was more straight forward, just tick a few boxes and that was that, not like now with these things." Skinny guy tapped the laptop.

"No I mean, should they be up there with the people they killed?"

"It's the whole forgiveness thing, God is big on it, otherwise everyone would be at each other's throats, bit like down here. You've got a lot of apologising to do to a lot of flies and spiders. Was the sixty one or sixty?"

"Sixty one."

"I gotta fill this in correctly or else they'll be all over my bony arse when I'm finished today."

"You look different from what I imagined."

"You were expecting the monk's habit and all that?"

"Um, yeah."

"We dropped it a while back, to be honest I was glad, you work ten hours in one of those things and you not only look like death, you smell like him."

"I can imagine."

"Not... nice... I can tell you." The skinny guy punched a few more buttons and then closed the laptop then looked and smiled at Chris.

"Is that it?" Chris looked back at his phone which still flashed Laura's name and then back at the skinny guy. He wished he had a photo of her so he could see her once more before he went. He regretted never having one on his desk, he regretted a lot of things.

"That's it; we are up to date on paperwork so it's time to go."

"Can I just..." Chris's voice trailed off because he didn't know what he wanted to do with his last moment, his mind splashed around like a drowning man and then he realised all the things he needed to do weren't as important as he'd once thought they were.

"Can you just what?"

"Can I just tell my wife I love her?"

"Didn't you do it at the end of the last call?"

"No... no I... I didn't..."

"Well man, I'm sorry, all I can say is... you should have."

Thanks.

I'm sitting here hoping you've enjoyed this collection of short stories as much as I enjoyed writing them. They are all true, the tears, the fears, the laughter and the years captured in several notebooks that, if we ever meet, I'll be happy to show you.

I'd like to thank several people whose support has made this book possible, so if you didn't like it, you know who to blame.

Firstly Angie Sammons, as I said in the foreword, without her help, and her magazine, this book wouldn't exist.

Next has to be Jo Hughes, her promoting my writing on various sites and twitter has brought me readers who would never have read. And her kind words have brought me confidence where there was occasional doubt.

Thanks Jo.

Broadcaster Ian Collins has to get a mention too, his re-tweets and kind words on websites and on air have shown me that a dream just might come true. If you've never listened to the guy, you really should do, he's not as good as me on the radio, but he's not bad.

I need to thank all my close mates, and ex police colleagues who have dropped me the odd line telling me to keep going, it has always helped and the wonderful people who have, over the years, commented on both Liverpool and Manchester Confidential magazines website saying nice things about my writing.

And finally I'd like to thank you, for reading it; I appreciate you taking the time.

Oh, and before I go, if you are ever in a taxi in Liverpool and the driver fancies a chat? Be careful, it might just be me...

Tony

18th April 2013.

At the very very tiny tips of my forefingers there is a universe.

You can't see it; in fact, no matter how hard I stare, neither can I.

But I know it's there.

It's an amazing place; anything can happen there, it grows out from the smallest digit like a huge balloon, getting bigger and bigger and bigger and bigger until it's the biggest thing anyone can imagine.

In it I can be king or a queen. I can be a horse, on a beach, or maybe jumping over a mountain. I can be mouse or a dinosaur, a murderer or a dead body or even a maggot in a dead body.

I can be one person, or a million.

Fight a war or plant a seed.

I can be a rock in a desert or under the sea or being broken by a prisoner who dreams of a girl he once knew in a small town that never was.

I can have dreams and wake up then go back and dream them again in a different colour.

I can be you or I can be your father or your father's father.

I could be the spider in the bath you killed last night, slipping and sliding gasping and rasping to my doom.

I can be now, or I can be then, I can be here, there or somewhere and I can be happy and I can be sad at the same time and then not at all.

I can laugh, cry, live, die and never have existed.

And when I've been all that, done all that, dreamed all that and seen all that.

I can give it to you and you can be it too.

All you have to do is read it.